How to Be Human

An Autistic Man's
Guide to Life

Jory Fleming

with Lyric Winik

SIMON & SCHUSTER

NEW YORK   LONDON   TORONTO   SYDNEY   NEW DELHI

Simon & Schuster
1230 Avenue of the Americas
New York, NY 10020

First Simon & Schuster hardcover edition April 2021

SIMON & SCHUSTER and colophon are registered trademarks of Simon & Schuster, Inc.

For information about special discounts for bulk purchases, please contact Simon & Schuster Special Sales at 1-866-506-1949 or business@simonandschuster.com.

The Simon & Schuster Speakers Bureau can bring authors to your live event. For more information or to book an event, contact the Simon & Schuster Speakers Bureau at 1-866-248-3049 or visit our website at www.simonspeakers.com.

Interior design by Carly Loman

Manufactured in the United States of America

10   9   8   7   6   5   4   3   2

Library of Congress Cataloging-in-Publication Data

Names: Fleming, Jory, author.
Title: How to be human : an autistic man's guide to life / Jory Fleming.
Description: First Simon & Schuster hardcover edition. | New York : Simon & Schuster, 2021. | Summary: "A remarkable and unforgettable memoir from the first man with autism to attend Oxford on a Rhodes scholarship, revealing what life is really like inside a world constructed for neurotypical minds while celebrating the many gifts of being different"—Provided by publisher.
Identifiers: LCCN 2020029847 | ISBN 9781501180507 (hardback) | ISBN 9781501180514 (ebook)
Subjects: LCSH: Fleming, Jory,—Mental health. | Autism. | Autistic people—United States—Biography. | College students—United States—Biography. | Autistic people—Social aspects. | Autistic people—Life skills guides.
Classification: LCC RC553.A88 F57 2021 | DDC 616.85/882—dc23
LC record available at https://lccn.loc.gov/2020029847

ISBN 978-1-5011-8050-7
ISBN 978-1-5011-8051-4 (ebook)

*To Mom—now the world can see
how much you have given me.*

Contents

1

Diagnosis: Autism

This book should not exist. Diagnosed with autism at age five, struggling with severe language delays, unable to succeed in a traditional elementary school, Jory Fleming wasn't expected to graduate from high school. There was no guarantee he could complete four years of college. The thought that he would be awarded a Rhodes Scholarship to study for a master's degree at England's prestigious Oxford University was practically unthinkable to almost everyone, including Jory himself.

Yet today, Jory has an MPhil from Oxford appended to his name.

This is not a happy-ending, motivational story or a step-by-step manual for how people with autism can achieve success. Jory is the first to say he does not want to be a poster child for autism or think he can provide an easy answer key to autistic understanding. "I'm certainly not expecting anyone to completely understand autism who doesn't have it. That's unreasonable. In the same way, I can't fully understand them. Even if two people who are very well-intentioned try to explain it to each other, there will be some things where both of us will shake our heads or shrug our shoulders and be like, I can't get there."

Rather, Jory's story is a window into what it is like to live in a world constructed for neurotypical brains when your mind is not. It is the story of what it is like to begin each day knowing that you are fundamentally different from every other person pouring coffee or tea into their mug. It is a memoir of life inside a gifted and disparate mind.

As Jory shares his insights into thinking and navigating in a neurotypical world, it may lead you to question basic assumptions about how all of our minds work.

The first few times I spoke with Jory, my brain hurt. Physically hurt, the way my muscles wince after moving stacks of heavy boxes or on that first spring afternoon when I dig too long in the garden. Twice, I had to stop; my concentration was shot, mentally following his train of thought was akin to swinging a pickaxe through a channel of my own brain that had closed over years ago, or perhaps had never existed. And yet I think those images and that exhaustion are as close as I can get, in my own words, to explaining what it is like for Jory when he engages with much of the outside world.

He speaks so powerfully about the mental energy required for him to move through his day, of the constant balancing act he must undertake to manage the sensory chaos produced by the human world and yet still have his mind remain open and engaged, rather than drained and shut.

It got easier, for me, and I hope for him. I became more adept at following his kaleidoscope of ideas. Our conversations were never linear; instead, they expanded outward and veered sideways without fixed destinations. I came to appreciate his abhorrence of small talk; he became grudgingly tolerant of my requests for lists of things, such as words that make sense to him and words that don't, which he found tedious, and I found illuminating.

Gradually, as our chats continued, I began to reassess how my own brain is wired. Are there some situations where it is far better to approach a problem largely devoid of emotion? How imperfect is language in communicating? How much weight should be given to words? How much information do we miss when we interact with a group in a crowded room? And still bigger concepts: What is culture? What is disability? Who has value? Should imperfection or illness or painful difference be scientifically edited out of our genetic code and of society at large? Should it not? What is the deeper meaning of birds? What is faith? Plus one sentiment that stopped me cold: "Because no human-generated space is going to be a safe space for me forever."

And most of all, how to capture that in a book?

The answer: let Jory speak for himself.

To that end, I sat with hundreds of transcript pages from conversations, many conducted over Skype, but some had on walks through the British university city of Oxford or seated on park benches, overlooking quaint English gardens, surrounded by the twitter of birds.

We would often circle back to the same topic weeks or even months apart, so I took the liberty of grouping related material in one place. I cleaned up the usual excesses of *likes*, *reallys*, *justs*, and half phrases, while leaving a few behind. I pruned back the many *thing*s and *something*s and general repetition where it hindered clarity. Since Jory's words flowed from conversations, I included various forms of prompts, whether a question, a transition, or an identifier to give some context and architecture and a bit of a sense of our back-and-forth. The beginning also contains a brief guide to brain science and the development of our scientific understanding of the human brain, to ground and contrast with Jory's depiction of how his own mind works.

You won't find Jory recounting extensive details from his childhood or his life before college in these pages. He doesn't remember much of anything, aside from a few stray images—a toy rocking horse that he found uniquely terrifying or a deep snowbank that he sank into. He also doesn't remember much about growing up with his older brothers, Arich and Tyler, or his younger sister, Lauren. He recalls his childhood friend, James, and his surrogate grandmother, Miss Nancy, who lived across the street in South Carolina, but very few specifics. Most of the other people that he encountered made no lasting impression on his memory.

The keeper of Jory's personal narrative is his mother, Kelly Fleming. She is the one who can relate the history of Jory's early years and his autistic spectrum odyssey. (She remains an integral part of Jory's life; she relocated with him to Oxford, England, to care for his medical needs and to make sure that Jory got any additional support he might require.)

Their story begins when Jory was six weeks old and nearly died from a kidney infection that progressed to meningitis. Kelly was in her fourth year of medical school in Lexington, Kentucky. It was her second day back in class when the babysitter called the school. Jory was having trouble breathing and was not acting right. A trip to the doctor became a trip to the local hospital, where he was diagnosed with a kidney infection. When Jory's head began to swell and doctors tapped his spine, Kelly was standing in the room. Where there should have been clear fluid in the needle, there was pus. He was rushed by ambulance to the University of Kentucky's teaching hospital and into pediatric intensive care. Jory had a raging E. coli infection in his bloodstream. In many babies that young, such an infection can be fatal. Jory survived, but his left side was weak, so he was sent to physical therapy at a child development center. At five months old, he had surgery to correct the defect that had caused the kidney issue.

By twelve months, he was being seen by physical, occupational, and even speech therapists. The therapists mentioned that his language development was very delayed. At a year, Jory had not progressed much beyond the preverbal skills of a ten-week-old baby. It was also clear that much of the outside world was intolerable to him. He had "sensory integration disorder," Kelly was told.

Jory was placed in ankle braces to help him walk—he still has leg braces for stability and relied on a walker for longer distances until he was nearly a teenager. He was also sent to a pediatric neurologist, who diagnosed Jory with mild cerebral palsy.

The doctor said one other thing to Kelly, which barely registered. He told her that after reading the reports from the child development center, "I would worry a lot more about these speech issues."

"At the time, that just went right over my head," Kelly says. "He was eighteen months old. I wasn't that worried. It seemed like all his problems were physical. Autism," she adds, "wasn't even out there in my mind."

The family moved to Indiana. In preschool, Jory refused to play with other kids. He would only sit in a stationary rocking chair. In playgroups, if another child snatched Jory's toy, he wouldn't react. After having two older, far more rambunctious boys, Kelly thought to herself, "Wow, he's really good."

When Kelly was pregnant with Jory's sister, Lauren, she had to rush to the Emergency Department and left Jory with a babysitter at a neighbor's house for six hours. "He is the best two-year-old I have seen in my life," the woman told her when she returned. "He was so good. All he did was sit on the floor with his little fire engine and spin its wheels."

At the same time, Jory's sensory issues grew worse. He hated anything squishy and anything that moved forward or backward. He would not ride a wheeled toy; he would not mash Play-Doh. In response, he screamed. After one particularly awful session when Jory was about three, an occupational therapist suggested Kelly take Jory to a psychologist who specialized in autism. Kelly recalls, "I was really, really mad. I thought, 'The poor kid has cerebral palsy, and that has nothing to do with autism.'"

Except Jory couldn't really communicate. He had started to say words, but the words made no sense to anyone but him. He would repeat words, or maybe part of a phrase from a commercial on TV, but he often did not string sentences together in ways that made sense to other people.

"I remember we had a little cassette player, and I would ask Jory, 'Do you want your music?' Usually he didn't say anything. But one night, he said, 'It's a cold night.' I answered, 'Yes, it is. Do you want your music?' and he said again, 'It's a cold night.' I finally realized that probably what he'd heard me do was say,

'It's a cold night,' and start the music. After that, if he wanted the music on, he said, 'It's a cold night.' He'd never say yes or no. I figured out that 'it's a cold night' meant yes. If I didn't get 'it's a cold night,' I wouldn't play the music because he didn't want it. His brain had put words together and made a connection, but it was a connection that no one else got."

Then there were the hours of screaming. Jory would arrange his toys, a card game on the floor, or Thomas the Tank Engine trains on a train table, and if anyone touched them or changed their order, he would scream for as long as five or six hours. He insisted the dining room chairs be pushed in an exact way. Nothing could comfort him. Kelly remembers one winter when there was snow everywhere. "There was no getting in your car and going for a drive. There was only go upstairs and try to cover up the sound. Really, there was nowhere any of us could go in the house where we couldn't hear the screaming." Jory's older brothers, Arich and Tyler, "knew something was wrong with Jory. But it was hard for them. They all had to give up a lot."

After many months of evaluations and a move to South Carolina, the diagnosis came back: autism.

Jory also had digestive issues, which are common for many kids with cerebral palsy, in addition to severe, self-imposed food preferences, a frequent hallmark of autism. He was given what was supposed to be a temporary feeding tube following a stomach surgery for reflux. But when the tube was inserted, it perforated Jory's intestine. He contracted another life-threatening infection and faced a long recovery. He still relies on a feeding tube for essential nutrition. Each day, he wears a light backpack that delivers a constant supply of nutrients via a thin, plastic line. At the same time, Jory was also diagnosed with mitochondrial disease. Found in nearly every human cell, mitochondria are the energy factories of the body, transforming oxygen and nutrition into the "power" source that allows humans to function.

As his medical condition stabilized and improved, Kelly focused on targeted developmental and academic interventions, a special school program, and occupational and physical therapies. Jory still was not speaking in intelligible ways and often not communicating with words. Instead, he learned to get a picture of a juice cup from a Velcro board and hand it to Kelly. "It had to be a picture on the picture board or else he didn't know how to ask for it. He could repeat the word *juice* and could say it but wouldn't use it to communicate that he wanted juice."

In South Carolina, Jory was enrolled in an autism program for kindergarten. After one year, however, the program disbanded, and Jory was mainstreamed into a regular classroom. He hated it. "When the bus would come to pick him up, he would just scream," Kelly remembers. At school, he often walked the halls with an aide. "It took me a while to learn that being around other kids seemed to shut him down entirely. He would withdraw into himself and want to get away. We had hit a real roadblock during those years," Kelly continues. "Everything was so stressful and upsetting to him. I can't imagine what it's like if you feel that the whole world is just bombarding you, and you are upset the whole time.

"Little kids learn so much by watching people around them, but he spent his time throwing himself on the floor and screaming. And after it was over, he still wasn't watching. Every small thing had to be taught to him in little, broken-up steps. Even today, a package that needs to be opened, or something that has to be put together, he has a really hard time with. Especially the more practical it is."

At age eight, at the start of second grade, Kelly decided to try to homeschool Jory. "When I started to homeschool him, he began to learn a lot faster and read a lot faster. I think the reading really helped with his speech development because he could see, Oh, these words go together to mean something." But she adds, "I can say things to him now, and he still doesn't understand what I'm saying. He doesn't process it. And he is aware of that. He tries to look at me, I'll tell him something, and I'll ask, 'What did I just say?' And he'll respond, and it will not be what I said." A central struggle was any type of sequential direction: "Telling him to go to the laundry room and turn the light on, we might get one of those things done. For a long time until well into the teenage years, I couldn't give him more than one instruction at a time." Those challenges continue today. Recently Kelly asked Jory "to see" if a store had something they needed. Jory returned empty-handed but assured Kelly, "Yes, they have it."

What clicked with homeschooling was the structure, but also the mental breaks. "It was very much at his own pace and what his mind could handle. When his brain needed a break, the learning stopped."

Kelly became not only Jory's sole teacher, but his therapy co-ordinator and the person who eventually pushed him beyond his comfort zone. She recalls having "to be on it all the time. Every moment was a teachable moment." And her every moment belonged to Jory. "It takes over your entire life. I couldn't have my career anymore. I didn't have a social life." She is also very clear that her route is not for everyone. It may not be feasible, nor is it necessarily the best solution.

"My best hope at one point was for him to finish high school. Then once I realized he was learning a lot and was able to take a couple of college courses in high school, I started to believe he could go to college, with support. I thought if he finished with a degree, I would be so happy. I never thought he would win a Truman Scholarship or a Rhodes Scholarship." Jory was awarded both.

Jory's intellect wasn't always visible, even to Kelly. "He's got some kind of ridiculous genius brain that is not shown to anyone," she explains.

One reason that Jory's brain stayed "hidden" was that he did not share his thinking in traditional ways. Until he was about eighteen, he did not enjoy speaking and did not want to engage in conversations. He thought of verbal communication as necessary only to "exchange information," otherwise, he "didn't see the point." But Kelly adds, "It never occurred to me that having autism could be a bonus later for high-pressure interviews. He doesn't feel the pressure. He can just block everything else out."

When he speaks, Jory is also, in Kelly's words, "brutally honest. He can't lie. He's going to give a very blunt, honest answer. He's not going to think about how to please anyone else or what they want to hear."

Jory *is* blunt and honest. But nuanced too. He holds strong views, but they are tempered by logic, rather than emotion. And he is highly capable of articulating multiple sides. He dislikes arguments—although he did not hesitate to dismantle a few of mine—gives no weight to passion, and is quite comfortable with seeing the hand of a Creator in our human world.

He is also acutely aware of his own perceived shortcomings, whether it is a lack of emotional acuity, a tendency to interrupt, or the need for constant vigilance to monitor what he says and how he says it, lest he risk offending, or as he puts it, "bulldozing" someone else. But there were times as I listened to him speak so critically of himself that my own heart ached for him, a twenty-five-year-old, who not so long ago could not find the words to ask for a cup of juice and could only string together "It's a cold night." Now he holds himself—and is being held—to a high standard of conversational perfection. He must navigate an increasingly fractious world where often, for many of us, each word must be weighed, measured, and be meticulously chosen.

When Jory and I sat together for an Evensong service in the Worcester College Chapel in Oxford, amid the centuries-old densely carved dark wood, with candles glowing, and a colorful, imaginary kingdom of painted plants and animals almost dancing on the walls in the flickering light, I listened to the chaplain recite the Lord's Prayer. As I heard the familiar phrase "Lord, forgive us our trespasses as we shall forgive those who trespass against us," I glanced sideways at Jory, leg braces steadying his calves and ankles, with his faithful service dog, Daisy, at his side, her body down but her head raised, watchful and alert. I doubt the early Christian Gospel writers who penned those lines could have conceived of them being read—in English—to an autistic man in the twenty-first century, in an age that sits on the cusp of genetic engineering and artificial intelligence and openly debates the quest for a more perfect human.

But here we are. Who among us will define the concepts of intelligence and perfection? And how? Those unanswered questions appear like a running stitch woven through Jory's and my conversations and this book.

I'd like to think that Jory came to enjoy, and perhaps even look forward to, our conversations, which traversed everything from the finer points of philosophy to our mutual dislike of the smell of geese poop. I know that I did.

In Jory's pages, in addition to a fair number of big ideas, we discuss such assorted topics as emoticons, pundits, manuals for college peer leaders, and role models. And through it all, he tells his own story: we delve into his perception of what allowed him to gradually surface and remain engaged for longer stretches in a neurotypical world.

"At least some part of me recognized that even though the world was not in any way set up for me and I did not like it in many instances, for whatever reason, I still wanted to be part of it. To be a part of it, you have to play by the rules that the larger system constructs. But you always have the freedom of your internal space, which you can cultivate apart from that."

This is a journey to that inner space. I am humbled and grateful that Jory has shared it with me. What follows in these pages are my very best efforts to share it with you.

2

Brain Space

For centuries, the heart was what mattered. Ancient Egyptian embalmers removed every organ but the heart, believing it to be the reservoir of all human intelligence and emotion. The Greek philosopher Aristotle, writing in the fourth century BC, agreed and proclaimed it to be the dominant organ in the body. He identified the adjacent lungs and outlying brain as merely secondary or "minor" organs, whose chief role was to cool the all-important heart.

Not everyone was convinced. Other early philosophers and physicians argued that the brain had its own intrinsic value. Hippocrates, who gave us the physician's Hippocratic Oath, identified it as the reservoir of "joys, delights, laughter and sports, and sorrows, griefs, despondency and lamentations," while the surgeon and philosopher Galen theorized that the brain was the seat of our "rational soul." He located our spiritual soul inside the heart and decided that our third soul, responsible for appetites and pleasure seeking, was housed in the liver.

More than two millennia later, the brain has superseded every *other organ. In a master feat of human engineering, this three-pound mass has evolved to fold over upon itself so that it still fits inside the confines of our skulls. Spread out and smoothed, the brain occupies roughly three times the surface area of its bony container. Its true size is comparable to a pillowcase (and how interesting that the place where we lay our heads is in fact head-sized). The brain is now recognized as the controller of every bodily function and every intellectual pursuit. It is what automatically ensures that our lungs breathe and our hearts beat. It processes sound and taste, sight and smell and touch. Every creative impulse and numerical calculation we make arises in the mind. Every word spoken and every memory stored begin in the brain.*

But what is our brain?

Starting with crude autopsies and continuing to today's high-resolution brain scans, researchers have identified three main components of the brain—the brain stem, which is responsible for basic bodily functions, including breathing, heart rate, body temperature, sneezing, coughing, vomiting, and swallowing; the cerebellum, which oversees muscle movements, posture, and balance; and the cerebrum, the largest section, which sits atop the other two regions. The cerebrum is the area known for having two hemispheres, right and left, and it manages our senses—hearing, vision, touch, smell, and taste—as well as speech, reasoning, emotions, learning, and fine motor skills. If we want to read a book, listen to an opera, or build a building, we need our cerebrum.

The cerebrum's surface has yet another name, the cortex. This is where the human brain develops its distinctive folds—the peaks and valleys that make it resemble a rugged landscape, or, alternatively, a shelled walnut. The cortex functions a bit like a communications grid, transmitting messages, information, and signals across and through the brain's various regions.

So now we have a structure, a hierarchy, and a communications system, but how does that all work? How do we see, smell, and taste, but also think and philosophize, remember and forget?

Only in the last two centuries have scientists identified specialized regions of the brain, each tasked with performing different functions. Before that, it was believed that the brain acted together as a whole—it also didn't help that early proponents of localization had some odd ideas. At the start of the 1800s, Dr. Franz Joseph Gall argued that the part of the brain responsible for memory was located behind and above the eyes because, as he noted, people with "good" memories had "bulging" eyes.

It took decades of cutting apart the brains of the deceased, often from those who had survived with varying degrees of brain damage from strokes, accidents, and injuries, as well as electrode and other experiments on animal brains, for scientists to develop a more accurate map of which region does what. (All of this is further complicated by the fact that the names for the various regions are mostly derived from the names of surrounding skull bones, so there is a lot of confusing Latin-based terminology. No one says, "memory zone"; instead, it's the temporal lobe.)

Established brain science has since subdivided the human brain into four lobes inside each of the cerebrum's two hemispheres. Each lobe has different responsibilities. For example, personality and judgment are two aspects ascribed to the frontal lobe, along with concentration and self-awareness, while the parietal lobe to-

ward the rear of the brain handles language interpretation, pain, sense of touch, and spatial perception. The occipital lobe below it interprets color, light, and movement to create vision, and the temporal lobe at the bottom is assigned, among its tasks, memory, hearing, sequencing, and organization. Contiguous to these lobes lie additional areas, which make up the association cortex and whose functions are still being unraveled.

What is certain is that for all this mapping, no two brains are exactly alike. The exact locations that oversee crucial activities vary from person to person, even if by less than a millimeter. Sometimes, they vary by a lot more. While most people's language and speech abilities are housed in the left hemisphere, more than one-third of people who are left-handed have some or all of their speech abilities located in the right hemisphere.

Inside our minds, the transmission of information also differs. We all have axons, a scientific term for nerve fibers, which conduct impulses and thus information among regions of the brain, but the pathways followed by these axons are not identical. We are truly all wired slightly differently. Perhaps very differently.

Two recent projects to produce neural imaging scans of children and adolescents who have been diagnosed with autism spectrum disorder show that their cortexes, the communication and processing hub, have more folds, called gyri, in specific regions of the brain than those of children and teens who are considered "neurotypical." Those with autism spectrum disorder also have differences in the thickness and thinness of various parts of the cortex. In other words, their brains appear physically different.

Which takes this book to its central place: let's put aside our own assumptions and step out of high-resolution imaging and the pulsing noise of the MRI machine and meet Jory Fleming, a brain of one.

"My 'in-group' is just me" is how he puts it. "I never feel like I can ever make assumptions about anybody, because every time I've tried to do so, it doesn't work very well."

In addition to the challenge of autism, Jory still must cope with the lingering effects of mild cerebral palsy as well as his metabolic condition, mitochondrial disease, which reduces his ability to fully process nutrients from food. Along with requiring a feeding tube to receive specialized nutrition, he is limited in what solid foods he can eat. (Interestingly, numerous medical researchers are now focused on the relationship between bacteria in the human gut, digestive issues, and autism, including the direct link between the intestinal system and the brain via the vagus nerve. This nerve transmits signals between the gut and the brain stem at the nearly supersonic rate of 100 milliseconds—far less time than it takes us to swallow or take a breath. In fact, medical science is finding possible new links between the gut microbiome and other diseases, such as Parkinson's, as well as an array of mental health issues and additional brain anomalies.)

Perhaps, then, it will come as no surprise that Jory opts to explain himself by beginning with the concept of a neurotypical versus an autistic "menu":

Jory Fleming on Jory Fleming:

JORY: I don't exactly introduce myself as "Hi, I'm autistic Jory. How are you today?" A lot of people don't know I am autistic. If I've known someone for a while, it will usually come out at some point. I'll also bring it up myself if it's relevant or if for some rea-son it impairs my ability to do a task in a group. But it's not what I say to people I'm meeting for the first time. It's not really useful information.

I also feel like it's different than having a physical "illness." You can address an illness. If you have cancer, you might be cured of cancer, depending on the type of cancer, of course. There's a possible future where that illness is not present. Knowing that fact changes your reaction; you immediately see an illness as a negative. You think, I'm not in a state of health because I have this illness. But with autism, this is just my state. There is no other state and there is no future possibility of a different state, so there's nothing more to think about. I certainly wouldn't want to wear a scarlet letter for autism so that everybody knows I have autism when I speak with them.

The best comparison I can make is that because of my meta-bolic condition, I've never tasted Hardee's Monster Thickburger, with one hundred and seven grams of fat, or a slice of triple choc-olate cake. I have no idea what they would taste like. I know that they exist, I've seen commercials, but I have no actual knowl-edge, no conception of what they are. But I also don't sit around thinking about Hardee's Monster Thickburger or a slice of triple chocolate cake. If I could eat them, perhaps I would think about them more. In that analogy, having autism as opposed to being neurotypical isn't a huge irritation. It's more like every now and again, you are reminded that everyone else gets the burger or the chocolate cake. You sit at a table and realize everyone else is ordering off a different menu and is able to share what they or-dered, while there is nothing on the menu for you. You think, Oh,

I'm not part of that. But it only happens now and again, and then you just move on. It's not helpful to dwell on it, because nothing will change; it's just the way things are.

LW: How do you describe yourself?

JORY: My Twitter bio says I'm an enigmatic and eccentric thinker. If I was describing myself and telling somebody more than just the sort of factual sequence of events, I would probably talk about that.

I'm a walking trivia storehouse. I love facts. I love reading the news, listening to podcasts, just absorbing stuff. I really like to see people thinking about large-scale world problems, environmental problems, social problems. I like to think that problems can be solved. I'm really interested in meeting other people that feel the same way.

I generally consider myself to be kind of a strange person. I like to have fun but not in the ways that other people like to have fun typically. I like to play board games. I like to talk about weird things. I hate small talk. I like to hang out with other people with similar lines of interest. I don't like meeting strangers. If you become my friend, you'll know that you're part of a small group but one that I value really highly. I like to meet people, but I don't like to call many folks my friends. I'm sort of a mixed extrovert and introvert in that regard. I don't necessarily mind meeting other people, but I like to choose who I spend time with.

If somebody is interested more in me, I might tell them about some of my disabilities. Although, if I was just meeting somebody, I don't think I would unless they asked. I also usually don't introduce myself as religious, but if somebody else likes to think about religion, then I do like to talk to people about that as well. But I don't like to lead off with that necessarily. Just because I say I'm religious, I won't try to convert you and that kind of thing. But if somebody else likes to talk about those things, I like to talk about them. I'm very curious.

I'd probably start by saying, I'm from South Carolina, family basics. Usually I would mention college because I'm meeting other people of a similar age at this point. Then I would talk about what I study and why I study that. If I like them, I can go on forever about that with no problem.

I would say something to the effect that I consider myself to be from South Carolina, and my family comes from Kentucky. I have two older brothers and a younger sister, and if somebody wants details, I would say I was homeschooled since the second grade, and my mom was my teacher for all that time. She was an excellent teacher. I wrote a lot in home school and got to find out what my interests were. I liked to play tennis, still do from time to time. In home school, I found out that I really liked geography, so that's what I decided to study, and it conveniently worked out that the school right down the road had one of the best programs for that, so I started at the University of South Carolina. I added marine science after I met my academic advisor and learned to love that as well. From that came my interest in technology and science and the world. That journey took me on some very unexpected paths. I applied for some scholarships and ended up in England.

I know the value of education from experience, and I recognize that between therapy and Mom homeschooling me, I had a lot of very active interventions in terms of educational assistance in that regard. On one level, my transition from nearly nonverbal to, you know, whatever this is, being over here studying on a Rhodes Scholarship, was not like me just flipping a switch in a room by myself in the dark. It was very much of a constructed experience, and I was not the one constructing it. In some cases, I was being helped along on the journey by Mom and many others.

That stands out really strongly to me because even though my memories of that process are not very good, I understand the effort involved, and it also really saddens me that not everybody has that support, but I think they should.

Jory's Journey:

How did Jory develop from being a child who dreaded getting on the school bus to becoming a fully engaged college student and a Rhodes Scholar studying at Oxford? How does he describe his personal journey? How does he talk about autism? And what does he think about the idea of "curing" it?

LW: Do you remember when you were told that you had autism? Or when you understood what it meant?

JORY: No, because there was never a moment where little me was at Dr. C's office and I understood what was going on. I vaguely remember weird things like tests and developmental checkups. I vaguely understood that she was not a "sickness" doctor but a different kind of doctor. When I was being homeschooled, I suppose I knew I had autism, but it wasn't until late middle school and high school when I sort of conceptually understood what autism was. When I started going to youth group at church, another guy there had autism. It was interesting because while he had autism, it wasn't the same; there were some differences and some similarities. So I sort of thought about it then.

My mom never really, at least to my knowledge, sat me down and said here's the exhaustive list of your conditions and what that means. There was never an information 101 session. I still have to ask her questions, and doctors often speak quickly when trying to explain things, which makes what they are saying more difficult to follow.

Over time with autism, there was a process of self-discovery, I suppose you could call it—although I tend to think less about autism, because my other disabilities are much more obvious and place more limits on me that I notice. The limits from autism at this point are very internalized. I know that I have no idea about emotions, and to compensate for that, I have tried to build filters to make sure I think an extra bit about what I am going to say so I don't accidentally stomp all over someone emotionally.

I can also still be unaware of the consequences of language, but at least I had a certain intention, and language I chose was very intentional. I may have made a really bad miscalculation in how it would be perceived, but it was still an active choice. Everything I do is active.

But to be quite honest, when I started college, I didn't really tell anybody that I had autism. Later on, some people that I had gotten to know relatively well because we were in student groups and saw each other very regularly in class, I would tell them. I came up with a brief description, because quite a number of people had not met or had only sort of secondhand met someone with autism. I had an elevator speech in which I tended to focus on how it's less comfortable for me to be in social interactions, that conversations could be difficult, and that I would miss things like social or body cues and emotional reactions and states—these are the things I'm not good at in particular. I kept it at a very summary level, because I thought it was helpful for people to know what I'm not good at so they wouldn't feel weird if a situation came up and I was acting differently. Before that, I didn't really think about what it meant to have autism. It just was.

LW: What made you want to engage with the world around you, to push through the barriers and participate and communicate?
JORY: Relatively early on, some part of me recognized that even though the world was not set up for me and I did not like it in many instances, I still wanted to be part of it. And to be a part of it, I had to be in control and had to play by the rules that the larger system constructs. It's hard work, but this is something that is valuable to me; it's going to mean increased engagement with friends and things of that nature, so I'm going to do it. There was also a recognition that if I don't have control and adverse consequences are happening as a result, the logical thing to do is attempt to gain some control.

But I feel like any ascribed motivations were pretty simple; there was no complexity. No deep philosophical impulse—"I think, therefore I am"—or anything crazy like that. It's more that there are some adverse consequences and I could reduce that.

LW: How did you "gain more control" over your brain as you grew older?
JORY: The difference back then was that autism was more in

control of my brain, I guess. I didn't respond well to much of anything. But autism now is different from autism then for me. "Suppress" has such bad connotations in this instance, but it unfortunately is the closest word that would adequately convey the broad meaning of what autism is for me now. It's still very present because of the way my mind works and the way I think and respond to things. But I make a distinction between parts of autism that I have removed or that I actively remove and the parts I don't.

I don't really adequately understand how other people with autism handle it. But I've always had a sense that some folks seem to have a more evolutional or merged approach, and then other people may be more similar to me, and we have more of a precision removal or suppression-based approach. But the end result is obviously very similar, so there can't be that much difference. In some sense, perhaps my approach to autism is merely a better understanding of myself, since everything is happening within the same space up there.

LW: When do you feel like you really became Jory—understanding that Jory is still a work in progress and who you are at age fifty-five will be different from now? When did you begin to have a sense of who you were?

JORY: I think I have a pretty good idea. I think there's two parts of me that I came to know. The first part was who I am personality-wise. I suppose I learned that in high school. And then I found out what I'm interested in and what I want to do with myself and got to know myself in that regard. Then I got to know myself in terms of how do I want other people to think about me, which is basically another way of saying how do I want to interact with people? I learned those two things in college. Both of those things I think are really important.

To know yourself is a very gradual process, especially because as you grow older that changes slightly. But overall, I think what helped me were points of comparison. Two things that I really liked doing when I was younger were reading and playing video games. Another would be nature, bird-watching in particular. What all those things share is observing actors in another story. You're observing all these actors. And I guess the process of self-discovery would be that, the way that my mind works, I build off of information. I wasn't interacting—I didn't like to interact with the people, to put it mildly—but I did have lots of points of comparison in terms of stories. Comparing myself to all these things (and to the people around me, of course) was particularly instructive. I discovered what my interests were through experience. That was really valuable.

For methods of learning, experience is valuable. For more abstract things, experience is helpful followed by visual stuff. I got to experience what I was interested in by taking two geography classes while I was still in high school and also shadowing a geographer to see what his job was like. I got to experience what the whole geography thing was about rather than reading the Wikipedia page.

Besides my interests, I learned more about my values by doing service activities. I also learned more about how to interact with others by doing leadership programs and being involved with other students and organizations, by participating in a shared activity. I was involved in two programs: one was a reading program, and then one was the Marine Science Club. For both, we went out to local schools. The reading program, Cocky's Reading Express, was a partnership between student government and the mascot program. The University of South Carolina mascot, Cocky, would read to little kids and act out books. The kids loved Cocky. They were fun and asked good questions. I signed up for tons of trips on the Cocky teams, where I would help by surveying classrooms, handing out books, sometimes being a reader, and also helping new volunteers. I also had the education outreach coordinator position with the Marine Science Club for a couple of years.

Doing these activities, I realized that I'm really driven by stuff that I want to see get better. I also recognize that I only have about forty or fifty years to make a difference. The clock's ticking. And you have to think of it like "the clock is ticking" if you are involved in education because you are passing down something to the next round of people, who in a weird way will one day become you.

Talking about Disability:

When Jory was selected as a Rhodes Scholar, he received national media attention. After an article appeared in the Wall Street Journal, *one of the online commentators wrote, "Maybe Jory will find a cure for Autism." I shared this quote as the framework for us to discuss Jory's thoughts on an autism "cure," as well as the larger question of what it is like to be disabled in a world that increasingly values the mentally and physically able.*

Beyond that discussion hovers the larger, philosophical ques-

tion of what it is like to navigate a culture that actively tries to
edit out what it perceives as imperfections. Consider the flawless
images of Instagram or the ability of programs such as Photoshop
to erase the most minor physical blemishes. What does that do to
our cultural acceptance of differences? In reply, Jory posed his own
question: Is it ethical to remove autism or is it unethical not to?

JORY: I get confused when researchers try to find cures to autism. It's like well, why? Nobody's ever said, "Why?" For someone
like me, where I do face a lot of challenges as a result of not being
able to order off the same menu [as a neurotypical person], I still
wouldn't choose to have a different menu after having lived with
this one. I'm really appreciative for the way that I think. Even if
I had new opportunities, I feel like I would lose as well. It's not a
win or a win-win—it's a loss. And I wouldn't like the losses. Some
of the benefits I wouldn't want to lose are not being able to be as
easily influenced by emotion and my memory. There are other
benefits, like methods of thinking; I seem to have more visual
thinking than other people, and that's a benefit.

LW: What do you think about the concept of someone wanting
to "fix" or edit out autism?
JORY: This discussion is also part of a broad, moral thought
that doesn't necessarily apply just to autism. Potentially in ten,
twenty years, it could apply to a whole bunch of different things.
With gene editing, for example, my concern is that we will ask
first, but think later. Not practical thinking, but moral thinking
or ethical thinking. Those elements are usually slower than technology. It takes time for philosophy to catch up with technolog-

ical advancements. My concern is that with biological editing, we change something before we understand what consequences would be bad. Not just trying to edit out autism, but all sorts of other things also.

It's a more interesting and nuanced question whether way in the future you could decide whether your kid had autism or not. Would it be ethical to have a child where there's nothing "wrong" with them, but they had more challenges because of how society is structured? I think that's an interesting question because in my mind, you have to be very clear about the fact that having a disability is not a problem under certain definitions—and certainly people with all sorts of disabilities interact and contribute positively to society, whether they have autism or something else. But you also can't deny that having a disability means having additional challenges in life. It is a really weird question to think whether autism could be removed completely or whether it would be unethical not to remove it.

Right now, there's a debate about whether to edit out— to kill—a bunch of mosquitoes that induce malaria by self-destructing an entire subspecies of mosquito. Scientists are conducting bio tests with a fake ecosystem to see what happens. I think that'll be a good precursor because humans get much more complicated. With gene editing, you'd be eradicating a "subspecies" of humans—not a subspecies biologically, but you'd be removing an aspect of the human experience, but for what benefit exactly? The benefit of removing malaria is very clear, but would removing autism actually benefit society? Should society change to recognize the benefits of autism instead of just the challenges? These kinds of questions need to be asked and thought about a lot. Certainly, my experience has been very challenging, and it has also been rewarding. And who knows, hopefully, I'll be able to do something with my life that benefits other people in some way.

What if that didn't happen? What if I didn't happen?

I don't know. I don't know how to do that cost-benefit calculation or whether you should even ever do a cost-benefit calculation on that kind of stuff.

There will always be the really strong moral question: Is it unethical to not do anything when you have the capability of removing troubles? I'm more worried than anything else that the simpler moral arguments that are easier to understand will carry more weight and will end the discussion prematurely. I worry that emotionally driven arguments will have more appeal than other arguments. I think it's really hard for neurotypical people to divorce decision making from emotions and social fabric.

The codes F84.0 and 299.00 are both medical diagnostic codes for autism spectrum disorder. They are how medical professionals categorize and quantify autism as a diagnosis and a disability. But how does Jory perceive disability? What is his experience living with both physical and cognitive differences? And how do other people respond to him?

JORY: In general, I feel like a lot of people are defeated by emotions or defeated by suffering. They experience it or see it and have an emotional response, and it's debilitating. It's disabling. But in a weird sense, I feel like my disabilities have shown me the opposite, that I see the good things.

I wouldn't want to get into a numbers game with anybody in terms of suffering, but if I had to do that, my numbers would be pretty high. I have more than one disability and you could argue that my life is not easy. But what matters is my response to that. Because I'm the one that's generating that meaning, I'm the one deciding on my response. And every other person has the capability to generate their own meaning and their own response. It's almost like my response to the human condition is the human condition. I know who I am, I am human. I feel like darkness will give way to light if you "light a candle." It may only be in a limited sphere. The light can't penetrate everything, but you should still light it.

Why There Will Never Be Jory's Ten Top Ways to Deal With Me, Which Can Be Universally Applied to Everyone with Autism

I can't make assumptions about other people, but other people tend to automatically make assumptions about me. Which, in all fairness, is hard because autism varies between individuals. It's not like you can read "Jory's ten top tips to deal with me" and that would apply to the next person with autism. Either they wouldn't, or some of them would, or you'd have to change some of them, or who knows. That's hard for people. That's why I think many people have an uneasiness about interacting with people that are different from them.

Whereas, if anything, I have the benefit because I'm uneasy interacting with everybody, so nobody can tell. Nobody notices because I've got the same level of uneasiness with everybody except for a very, very few number of people.

LW: Would you prefer it if people asked you more frequently about autism if they were curious? Or is not discussing the topic fine?

JORY: I think it depends on whether or not it is sharing useful information. As far as with friends, I think it might be beneficial if they brought it up more because they might learn something about autism which they didn't know. I don't feel like I'm losing out on anything by not talking about autism, but perhaps other people might be.

Talking about Autism:

Jory explains his autism using a hand-drawn map, a Goya etching, and a magician.

Autism is not a routine discussion topic for Jory. He prefers not to talk about it, but he is strikingly thoughtful about describing the architecture of his brain and the mechanics by which it operates.

At the University of South Carolina and at Oxford, Jory majored in geography. Geography these days is about far more than the study of maps, but mapping remains part of its core. One of the first things I asked Jory was to make me a map of how he envisions his mind, from which we could then set out into the general topography of his world. Looking at this map, I was struck by how much it resembles a mandala, a ritual symbol in Buddhism and Hinduism that represents the universe.

JORY: I drew a circle with a lot of lines going everywhere. I didn't draw any of these lines to be straight because I feel like nothing in my brain is especially straight. The larger outer circle is where I envision the conceptual me might rest. The objects on the edges are databases for storing memories or facts or whatever. I am

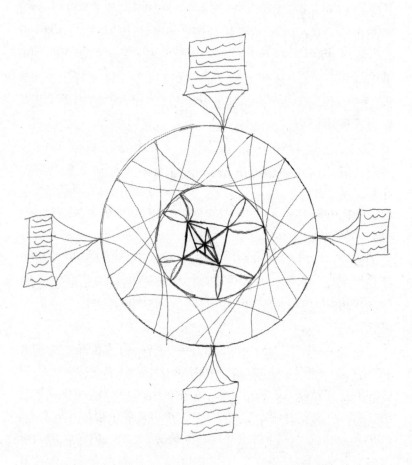

located inside, and I pull them in. The second circle in the middle is like a theater—that's where I look at shards of memory or facts. Whenever I want to do something with my thinking process, I'll push the information I need into the middle space so I can visualize or translate it into other mechanisms, like speech. I imagine these outer databases are probably similar to how other people's brains work, but then inside my mind, it all kind of goes everywhere. The conceptual me is moving really, really fast in a circle around and around, until I get to a point where I pick up what I need and push it into the inner circle.

The reason why I thought of a circle was because it offers the most space of any shape to move around in. I'm also influenced by the movie *Arrival*, where the aliens speak in ink circles, and small differences in the circles mean different things. The movie is about how scientists try to communicate with the aliens. What's hilarious is the aliens don't actually do anything for most of the movie. They just sit and draw these weird circles, while the scientists try to figure them out. The military and political leaders are freaking out; they are about to blow up the aliens and each other because they can't understand the circles. And in reality, the aliens are just chilling. Which is a decent metaphor for me, because that's how I feel about other people sometimes—it's like I'm simply drawing circles, and no one else can figure them out.

I also made a weird shape in the middle. I don't know why I drew it as a double pyramid, but I felt like another circle isn't quite right because that space is a bit more constrained and angular. It's where I translate my thoughts into words. I think of language and speaking as linear. So I have to translate my thoughts and ideas into a more rigid or angular way in order to communicate because most people have a linear brain. I definitely don't.

My mind doesn't move from A to B to C, and that could be one reason I'm pretty terrible at following directions sometimes. Most people go from A to B, because it is the easiest way to do something, but I don't. I go from A to Q.

For many years growing up, I didn't have complete access to or control over my brain in the way I do now. I spent a lot of time trapped in the midlevel space, where I was receiving stimuli from the environment, but I didn't have access to the inner circle's resources. I couldn't translate it into "Jory form"; I couldn't think; I just shut down and wasn't able to do anything.

Jory's follow-up answer to what an autistic brain looks like was to share a lithograph, Goya's The Sleep of Reason Produces Monsters. *It is not the sleeping figure that he is drawn to or the title, but rather the creatures in the background. "They seem," he said, "as if they are part of a different world, that they are operating in a different sort of system."*

JORY: At first it looks like the person is the center of the story, but the actual center is the thing that looks like a cat, or some animal. It's staring directly at the viewer. For me, it's like a visual representation of autism, being kind of beneath the surface.

Autism is part of my mind, but I don't think it's the most important part of my mind. I like to think of my brain as machinery that was crafted by autism, even though I consider myself the

operator now. But autism is still technically at the center. And with this particular piece of artwork, what's in the center is also beneath the surface.

Most of us may be nominally aware that our brains are divided into two hemispheres—a left and a right brain, analytics and emotion, but Jory conceives of his brain as divided between the brain machinery that he understands, "the brain machinery that

I am now at the helm of," and a second part that he does not understand and that remains an inaccessible mystery.

JORY: I think a good part of my brain is always dealing with
autism. It's not accessible because it's occupied doing something
more important than what I want it to do. It says "Busy." I envision autism as being like a magician sending lightning bolts,
while the other part of my brain is a wall builder, adding bricks in
multiple layers. One layer gets smashed by the lightning bolts, so
my brain has to build it back up again. If I'm in a stressful environment, more lightning bolts are coming in, and the builder has
to work faster. More of my brain resources have to be devoted to
building.

Why a magician to represent autism? That is a part of my
brain I don't understand, it's mysterious to me, and magicians
are very mysterious. They have cool robes and stuff, which make
them extra hard to get a handle on. I also have the sense that
what I want to do in my mind is not aligned with what the magician wants to do—and the magician is unhappy about that, thus
the lightning bolts. It's almost like at certain points the magician
is charged up because of the environment.

LW: When did you realize you needed a wall to contain the magician and his lightning bolts?

JORY: I think when I was younger, the situation was reversed,
the magician was at the helm. I was on the outside looking in;
I was not at the helm. But at some point, I reached a kind of
a weird equilibrium, roughly equivalent to when I began to interact more with the world. As I grew, I feel like my standing in

relation to autism changed until at some point the roles were reversed. In college, I got to the point where autism was less something that I had to be concerned about on a day-to-day basis. I was much more confident in being able to withstand a complex environment and have the wall hold.

I think it's also a question of what do you define as autism? Is it the state of my brain or is it the responses that I can't control, the times when the other operator takes control of myself away from me? In which case, I can try to suppress that. I'm not always successful—I'm successful on a core level, but on a superficial level I have to pick my battles.

I think most people have a very poor idea of what autism is because they don't have experiential knowledge. But from my perspective even with experiential knowledge, it's hard to explain because I don't know what it is either. In my case, I feel like the paradox between the magician and the wall builder is what enables my brain to exist now in an extremely stable state. It's an unresolvable problem, and that creates stasis, which is a pretty decent word because it lacks a lot of connotations that are positive or negative. And the result is me. But I prefer to use images because words are incomplete; pictures might give more flavor and fewer connotations.

Talking about How Jory's Mind Works:

It's not simply that Jory perceives differences in how his brain functions, it is that he perceives differences in terms of how he functions compared to other people. Most of those differences revolve around the absence of language.

JORY: I'm increasingly aware of the cognitive distance I can feel sometimes with other people. What I see or what I interpret are different from how other people usually interpret the same thing. I also think that many times people claim to be presenting objective information, but they are really transforming it into subjective information.

For instance, I think other people look and say, "Oh, that's a tree," or "Oh, that's a book." Whereas for me, I'm actively interpreting the information I see—I'm pulling out past recollections of trees, not doing some kind of word association. There's no need for me to use language.

I never talk to myself. It would take way too much time for me to have an internal discussion with myself. When I think about stuff, I just think. Why would I talk to myself? I'm pulling in the information I have stored, then I just combine those pieces or throw them up in my mind to look at them.

LW: Here's an image-based mental-processing analogy for you to try: Let us imagine that all these pieces of information are Lego bricks. To build something using the Lego bricks, a neurotypical person would most likely think, "I'm going to pick up the yellow Lego brick and attach it to the red Lego brick. Next, I'll attach a blue one and scale up from there." What would you do with the bricks? How do you envision them? And are Lego bricks even the right analogy?

JORY: I think it's a good analogy with the exception that I think Lego bricks are too rigid and sequential. You can still use the Lego bricks, but just imagine tossing them all up. It's as if there is no gravity, the Lego stays frozen and suspended, and you can float in the middle. And you don't need to actually build anything, you can just spin around and observe all the Lego bricks and maybe draw lines to connect where they would go. You could see it, without building anything. The Lego bricks would remain in the same place and not be sequential. Instead, they can make any number of combinations. Maybe a better analogy would be Play-Doh bricks, so they can change shape, because if I decide it's no longer useful for the Lego brick to look like a Lego brick, then they no longer do.

One reason that Jory finds language to be limiting and confining is because he finds language inherently imprecise and subjective.

After our Lego brick discussion, we returned to talking about the Goya etching—and the subjectivity of most verbally based human thought. This led us to a longer discussion on subjectivity and objectivity in language and thoughts. Our back-and-forth also illuminates how Jory categorizes information in his own mind.

JORY: I was thinking about the etching and how people like to think that parts of their mind are objective. But the way I see it, it might not be possible to escape subjectivity, which is really interesting to me. I've always been confused by things like culture, worldview, or any ideology, because it's as if people think one of those Lego bricks is always more important than another Lego brick. Even if it's true for you a certain percentage of the time, it still does not negate the other percentage of the time where that one Lego brick is not more important.

I find it very confusing that people can have ideologies or worldviews that add another layer that constrains their thinking.

From my point of view, having an ideology has to constrain your thinking because often you can't treat an opposite ideology in a neutral way. You might respond to an opposite ideology with emotion and react strongly. Whereas in my mind, that doesn't make sense. Like, why would anyone do that? For me, having a reaction just because another person says something that I disagree with wouldn't occur. It confuses me where these emotional reactions come from.

That additional layer is just as problematic for me as the language layer. I don't grasp the nuance and the shared understanding, which everyone else recognizes intuitively.

Why the Concept of Culture Does Not Make Sense to Jory:

JORY: It definitely doesn't make any sense to me at all. Why does growing up in this place mean you speak in a certain way and have certain views and ways of thinking? In my mind, there should be no difference, if you basically speak the same language, as in the United States and the United Kingdom. However, a difference in the landscape is very clear and easily understandable to me, like differences in topography and climate. That's the only thing I can try to use to understand: How do these different features of the landscape influence culture?

At one point, Mom and I were visiting Northern Ireland on a tour. We could look across the Irish Sea and see Scotland. It was only fourteen or fifteen miles away. But if you cross the water, there'd be differences, and that really does not make any sense to me. They're so close together; they should be the same, but they're not.

LW: I'm going to flip that idea: you talk a lot about your own deficits, things that you think you do not do well. But I listen to you talk about culture, and I find those ideas refreshing. The concept that you and I wouldn't treat each other any differently because we might come from two different cultures is a positive, not a negative, to me. What do you have to say about that?

JORY: There are both good and bad things that come with any perspective. A lot of people talk about diversity as a buzz-word. But if you look at the benefits of, say, biodiversity, part of its strength is due to its complexity, which includes both the strengths and weaknesses of everything around us.

For instance, you may find my perspective on culture to be refreshing because it's different. But from my perspective, I also see that while a cultural argument is not really going to hold weight with me, I can recognize that autism could also be considered a minority group. And for other minority groups, especially ethnic minority groups or religious minority groups, their culture is very important and is actually part of their different perspective.

Ironically, culture, the thing that I consider not making any sense to me, is very important to those individuals and also has larger value. So there's a paradox: my perspective says this has little value, but their perspective says it has a lot of value. Most people seem to have a problem accepting that a paradox can exist because they are under some impression that their view has to win in order for progress to occur. I feel like people need to upgrade their thinking to handle those paradoxes and complexities a little better.

I also hope nobody thinks my perspective is particularly valuable just because it's different. I hope people see it, think about it, compare it back and forth, and get more nuanced about it. I'm certainly not expecting anyone to completely understand autism who doesn't have it. That's unreasonable. In the same way, I can't fully understand them. And even if two people who are very well-intentioned try to get as far as they can in explaining it to each other, there will be some things at the end where both of us will be shaking our heads or shrugging our shoulders, and be like, I can't get there. I don't mean that in an arrogant way. It's just, you don't understand some things, in the same way that I don't understand things about you.

But that's fine. And that doesn't also mean that we can't have a shared vision or act collectively toward a goal or basic things that people need to do.

On the issue of the inherent subjectivity found in language, Jory poses the following question: If you use language to think, do you really have your own thoughts?

JORY: I look at that etching, and I wonder if people really have their own thoughts, because if you use language to think, by definition you are using something that has not been fully constructed by you. In my view, language always has some elements of subjectivity because it's limiting. For example, in some Inuit languages, there are many words to describe forms of snow and ice. I recently heard about the incredibly precise Gaelic phrase *rionnach maoim*, which means "the shadows cast on moorland by clouds on a sunny day." All those specific words and phrases open more possibilities for sharing objective information. Whereas in the places I've lived, most people have only one way to refer to snow, unless you use a ridiculously long string of adjectives to precisely define the type of snow. But I think of that as a huge waste and also constraining. I think it limits objectivity. It's more difficult for me to translate and conjure a picture.

Add worldviews and ideologies to that, and are you even thinking on your own? Or are you drawing from multiple pots of information and don't even realize it? Whereas with me, when I go into the storage cabinet, even if I can't find something I want, I don't pull out anything by mistake. Let's say I throw all the red Lego bricks up and then a yellow one appears for no reason. I would not treat that yellow brick as more important because it's yellow. But it seems to me that is what people are doing with words, ideologies, and culture.

LW: What is objective information? What is subjective information? How do you define the difference?

JORY: I think of information as being like an instrument reading, something you can see and directly experience through your senses. But anything that goes through another human mind I consider to be subjective information. By that measure, another person's statement would be subjective information. Not that I don't trust that statement and information, but it's different.

Other people seem to have a much broader definition of what

makes information subjective or objective—and how you decide to classify something often depends on what you might have previously believed about that topic. Whereas for me, subjective and objective are very binary categories, depending on whether I've observed it myself or not.

I never feel like I can ever make assumptions about another person, because every time I've tried, it doesn't work very well. But I notice that sometimes other people automatically make assumptions, without ever thinking about it. It's almost like they forget that they hold their own ideologies, and I think that can create distrust. Whereas, from my perspective, it's not that I distrust people, but I don't assume things about them.

Repeatedly, what stood out in our conversations was how much Jory perceives himself as a singular individual, not part of any particular group or community. It is a double-sided impression: one of both individuality and also isolation. Above all, Jory has a profound sense of being different from everyone else around him. It's a theme that we will return to in a variety of forms.

LW: We've talked about how your brain is organized and some about how it approaches information. Let's talk about how it puts together that information. How do you think?
JORY: Nobody can really understand how I think. Their basis of comparison is themselves and other people who think neurotypically. But this also means that in many situations, I can potentially bring something entirely different to the table. I can even say the equivalent of why are we focused on a table, why aren't we talking about a carnival? Everybody else will be like,

"Whaat?" But that is the way I see things. I see things from an entirely different vantage point and on an entirely different plane.

I'd be the first to say that I'm very limited in what I can do that other people are good at, but the same is true in reverse. The small number of us out there who think differently, whether it's from autism or some other reason, might have something valuable to bring to the discussion. We can have a real benefit.

There are going to be positives and negatives. I try to take advantage of what I can. I also try to recognize the gaps, like the commonsense holes, which I will never be able to fill in. And then I try to use the benefits.

LW: What are those "commonsense holes" that confound you? What are the everyday tasks that you find hard?

JORY: That's a good question. As far as things that I sort of struggle with, one of them is definitely when I'm told something, and it's extremely short-term and extremely simple, and all I have to do is remember it. I have trouble with that.

For instance, Mom might give me a list of four or five things, and each one is an incredibly simple thing. Like pick up almond milk at the store or do the dishes. These tasks are not challenging. You think if you're given a list, especially a small list, it would be easy to remember. But actually, it's really hard for me to remember, and I think the reason why is, there's nothing for my brain to connect it to. There are no other pegs I can use to connect it to other parts of my brain, the way I can with facts or ideas and objects. I'll remember to do two out of the three things. My brain will think, Oh, I did all the things that Mom wanted me to do, but in fact I didn't because one of them just fizzled out, for lack of a better term. And that is pretty frequent.

I'll go to the corner store and get something Mom had requested a few days prior, but not the almond milk she requested that morning. I also have a hard time with things involving tools. I'll be doing something, and there will be a much easier way to do it, maybe by using a different tool or the same tool but in a different manner, and I just don't see it. It's like once my brain sort of sees a solution to the problem, even if it's a difficult solution, I'll keep doing it, where most other people would think, "Oh, that's not working. Let me try something easier." I'll be like, Well, this is only going to take me twenty seconds, so I'm just going to do it. But Mom will be able to do it in five seconds. I'll wonder, Why didn't I think of that? Most people think of many solutions to the problem and pick the best ones. My brain's more like the first-come, first-served approach, especially with tools.

Sometimes the sequence in which I do tasks doesn't make sense either. For example, if I'm taking out the trash, it might make sense to first take the trash inside the house out to the trash bin, and then take the full bin to the street, but I might flip those tasks. I'll take the bin out and then I'll walk back inside and back out again with the additional trash, adding an extra trip. I don't think about logical sequencing in simple tasks. I just sort of do the simple tasks in any order.

LW: What about simple tasks versus more complex tasks? Which are more difficult for you?

JORY: Generally speaking, most people seem to find simple tasks not particularly draining, but they find higher-level tasks or thinking tasks to require more energy. I'm the reverse. I find simple tasks really draining, while thinking tasks are not really draining for me. A good example was when I transcribed interviews that I did for my master's thesis at Oxford. It's just listening and typing, but I feel like it was one of the hardest things I've ever done. It wasn't hard. The recordings are extremely clear. But because it was just typing, it was really difficult for me.

The people I interviewed had to look at a bunch of maps and answer questions about what they had seen, about numbers and colors and various features on the maps. It took about an hour and fifteen minutes to complete the interview and study the maps. When I asked them about the experience, many times they said it was surprisingly tiring because they had to look at maps and think about things. I noticed enough of these comments to realize that people find it draining to think about mini-statistical graphics problems for over an hour, whereas, if you were to give me that test, at the end, I would say, "Oh, we're done? Where's more?" because I wouldn't have found that task draining at all.

I think most people, when they think about autistic people having difficulty with simple tasks, they assume it's because of incompetence. It's almost difficult for them to imagine that a simple task may in fact be draining for me in much the same way that they find complicated tasks draining.

It's not my personal preference for this to be the case. It certainly would be more convenient if simple tasks were simpler, but alas, it's not to be.

When Jory speaks about his struggles with commonsense activities, part of that challenge comes from his larger issues with lan-

guage. Here, he explains his thoughts on why basic directions often
don't make sense to him and do not achieve their desired result:

JORY: One reason why I'm bad at commonsense things is because my brain operates weirdly in the sense that it goes in various directions, which could be very helpful for more complex
things like thinking about systems but is very bad for like how to
screw in something.

I think it's helpful to explain in terms of ideas. Some people
think that an idea is a real thing. But I don't treat any ideas as real
in the sense that they're just little things that toss around in my
head. I also don't line them up. It seems to me that most people
think in a very linear way, like there's an idea, there's an opposite
and there's a line in between them. But why is it a line?

People seem to think that making their thoughts or ideas
more complex is all about making their linear systems more linear. They define their idea carefully and define its opposite just
as carefully. And then there's a linear equation which connects
them. And then multiple ideas intersect with other ideas to make
a system of ideas. But I just throw my ideas in all sorts of directions, until it's almost like there's no direction anymore. Visually,
it looks like trucking in a load of ideas, dumping it, and seeing
what happens. That process is what makes my mind terrible with
doing things simply or quickly or efficiently.

This is why I do not excel at linear directions, even simple
ones. I almost have to think through them more, which is ironic.
Usually I try to organize the things I need to do first versus second
because of deadlines. But Mom will tell you that I'm not very good
at that system because a lot of things get jumbled around, espe-

cially because I have a terrible habit of automatically deciding relative importance. My brain will just kind of shred things without my noticing, like I remember the first bit of Mom's instructions of what she wanted me to do and the last bit, but not the middle.

It's like because my thinking is much less structured, then applying structure is harder. I think this makes it harder to explain my thoughts as well. Sometimes I can't find the right word.

LW: A significant part of school, work, and even life revolves around following directions. How have you adapted to that—or have you?

JORY: Some people may look at where I am now and assume that I have adapted to the exterior world surrounding me, whether it's school, work, or something else. But I haven't really. Living in a linear world will always warp my mind into a shape that it doesn't belong in.

I was fortunate because, in the beginning, being homeschooled meant my education was adapted to me. If the suggested assignment was a word search, I was incapable of doing that—I still can't today—and Mom would simply replace it with something else. Having that freedom to learn in my own way gave me an ability to manage later in academic environments that were not built for the way my mind works. For instance, by the time I was in group science labs in college, I had the role of doing math calculations or double-checking group work rather than pipetting, which I am terrible at because of my limited fine motor skills. I could compensate for someone else's possible weaknesses, and they could compensate for mine. I've taught myself to take notes, but things like due dates have never been my strong suit.

And it really helps if I have a variety of ways to access directions. There are always going to be differences; the point is to find ways to build positive experiences and to combine strengths.

Talking about Autism, Specifically, What If Your Child Is Diagnosed with Autism?

Jory was very upfront about sharing his thoughts regarding an autism diagnosis. Our conversation also included the topics of emotions, labels, and feedback, and Jory's understanding that many neurotypical people experience feedback (and emotions) very differently from him.

LW: What would you say to a parent whose child has just been given the diagnosis of being on the autistic spectrum?

JORY: At the danger of sounding really cold, I don't think there should be too much of an emotional reaction. Because I see emotions as generally unhelpful, and this is probably an instance where emotions are unhelpful. Which I know is not what people want to hear, so I probably wouldn't say it to someone's face.

In this scenario, with a diagnosis of autism, I would hope that as things get more normalized and the family becomes more familiar with autism and has more context for autism—that their first reaction maybe wouldn't be that negative and certainly not negative about the child in particular.

Recognizing that there's a lot of uncertainty about the future, wondering what they will need to learn to be a good parent, things like uneasiness or confusion, those types of negative emotions are fine. That element of change is mixed in with like yeah, I'll have to change as well. But others, if it changes your view of the child, for instance, are probably unhelpful. If it's a nuanced and balanced emotional approach to this new situation, then that's fine. But a lot of times people's emotions are not terribly complex and nuanced. People say, "This all flew out of my mouth before I had time to think about it." From their perspective, they can't control what they feel.

Although maybe some people can.

In Buddhism, control of the self, removal of the self, is a huge thing. Some people can to varying extents, but that's different than the way I think about it, in terms of just removing it. But it's possible to acknowledge someone's response without agreeing with the response. I would acknowledge any response, but then I would be most concerned to make sure it's not negative, such as "Now I think my kid is less," whatever "less" means.

I also feel labels are particularly unhelpful, because labels get you to think about so many other things which may not have happened yet. If all you have heard about autism are horror stories, then that's going to be what you think about. Maybe you have fear. And you will probably think, "This is going to be me." I find that hard to understand, because the child—who that child is—has not changed after receiving a diagnosis.

From my understanding, raising a kid is really difficult regardless of whether or not they have autism. It was already going to be a pretty rough go. I am very uncertain about ever having kids. I do appreciate kids. Their questions are very direct, and they are smarter than many adults think they are. I also love working with kids, and I'm particularly interested in children's education issues, not necessarily because they are easy, but because I think they are important. But I've seen enough to know that raising kids in any circumstances is a really challenging thing to do.

Emotional Responses

One of Jory's more extended discussions of other people's propensity to give emotional responses was embedded in our conversation about an autism diagnosis and what he would say to a parent of a newly identified autistic child. Of particular resonance is his distinction between "what people need to hear" and "what they want to hear."

JORY: I know there is a lot of value in responding to people in a positive way, even if it's not what I think. For me, it's also really hard to distinguish what people need to hear from what they want to hear. Because emotions play into that so much. The correct answer might not be what they need to hear, because of the emotional element.

If you give somebody who is emotionally invested in a problem a critique, it's shocking to me that their response to the critique is almost always negative. Because if you told me there's a better way to do things, I would love to hear it. Because that means I can do it the better way the next time. And if it's not clearly a better way, then I'll go back and forth with you as to why you think it's a better way and why my way was worse. I would not have an emotional response beyond being slightly disappointed. I put some time and effort into it, but I'm not emotionally invested.

But for a lot of people, you have to think about how to give feedback. Bosses have to think about how to give feedback in a constructive way, but what's constructive isn't always going to be the most helpful, which is confusing to me. Because you'd think that in situations where emotions were not helpful or where they clouded judgment, people could just snap them off. But that's not really how things work.

LW: Any thoughts about therapies designed for autism, based on your experiences?

JORY: With regard to parents and various types of therapy, it's really challenging for anyone to say you should do this, but you shouldn't do this. Mom tried lots of things, and for me, certain therapies were effective, even if I did not enjoy them. But others didn't help, I did not respond well to them, and it was clear that I wasn't going to respond well to them after repeated attempts. For someone else, the balance of effective versus ineffective types of therapy or experiences might be different. I think parents would be well served with getting a variety of information and to try things out. And there's the bit about balancing the needs of the family.

LW: What are some of the broad misconceptions or generalizations that you see about autism?

JORY: I think there are two kinds of misconceptions that I tend to see. A lot of people don't understand that autism affects individuals in different ways. They might assume, based on their friend or a friend's friend who has a kid with autism, that all autistic people have significant mental challenges. I think many neurotypical people tend not to be aware of those people with autism who are contributing at different levels in society. I feel as if there are quite a number of people in the workplace who have autism but may not have had it officially diagnosed or choose not to share it with others.

I don't really know or understand very well the differences in how autism affects people. A lot of that is because I don't understand people in general. Some smart medical researchers may actually figure out reasons for some of these differences. What I do notice from my own informal sampling over the years, is that in different contexts, when I've met many people on the spectrum, they all think differently than me. Just as one neurotypical person may think differently than another.

The other misconception that I see a lot is the stereotype of people with autism being super socially awkward and doing strange things, having trouble with conversations, being emotionally challenged. There was a Netflix show called *Atypical*, about a kid with autism who's trying to find love or something like that. I didn't think it was a very good portrayal of autism because it focused too much on common stereotypes. You could tell they had done research to develop the character, but it came off as somebody who had researched and found all of the characteristics of autism and then the actor just amplified all of them, which is not really how autism works.

For me, I have those things, but at different times and different amounts. Mom and I also found it hilarious that they seemed to miss one key thing. The whole setup of the show is that this person is trying so hard to make romantic connections, and they didn't even fully seem to question the fact that maybe an autistic person isn't super up for that in the first place. For me, I've been on a few dates, but compared to other people, especially my age, I feel like it's a lot lower on the priority list for me, in terms of needing or wanting a romantic connection.

That Netflix show took a person's struggle and had all the stereotypes of autism causing problems, where because of these stereotypes, the lead actor couldn't seem to do what other people did. Just focusing on the outward characteristics is a surface-level approach, and it leads to more generalizations, in effect saying, "All autistic people are like this." Autism is far more than a collection of outward differences.

In fact, the one thing that I've noticed about autism—and I don't feel like I can describe it very well—is there are just so many individual differences at a deeper level. Some of those broader characteristics do apply in vast generalities to people with autism, but in different ways or different amounts, and in different environments. There's a lot of complexity that makes it difficult to try to pin down anything. The one blanket statement that I can make about autism is that there is no blanket statement to be made about autism.

LW: You don't like being called a role model for autism. Why is that?

JORY: I feel like autism is on a spectrum for a reason. In my mind at least, there's a wide variety of types and levels of impact on people with it. I've been asked questions like "What do you think about being a role model for autism?" One, I don't think role models are always a good idea, because everybody is unique, and everybody can be their own leader. Two, each person on the spectrum is different. Not every autistic person is going to excel academically, just like not every person is going to excel academically. It's in no way a negative statement; it's just a recognition of the huge variety of types and levels of impact. Different people excel at different things. It adds another layer of reasons why you shouldn't make generalizations.

3

Energy and Memory

Talking about the Energy Consumed by Autism:

A central topic of Jory's and my conversations was energy—
specifically mental energy. This is not the proverbial and perhaps
all-too-familiar "I'm feeling tired and sluggish" type of energy
drain. Instead, Jory is acutely aware of his brain's energy reserves,
the way a long-haul trucker must pay close attention to the gas
gauge. What he said sent me to research basic facts about the
human brain's energy consumption.

Our brains use more energy than any other organ, roughly 20
percent of the body's total expenditure. About three-quarters of
that energy is used to help neurons send signals, but neuroscientists believe the balance is most likely used for cell maintenance,
performing basic tasks to keep the cells healthy and function-
ing. It is the mental equivalent of doing laundry, washing the
dishes, and tidying up. Most of us probably do not think about
how much energy our minds require to operate, but Jory does,
every day.

This energy use is also directly related to Jory's external environment.

JORY: I'm always conscious of having to keep autism in a corner, and I have to divert mental energy to do that. I imagine a big switch located at the entrance to my mind labeled "important," and immediately, via that switch, a set amount of energy is shunted off inside my brain from the moment I wake up. That energy demand changes with the environment. If I'm at home, I just need to meet the minimum threshold. But if I'm out and about, the amount of energy I need to maintain that inner mental balance changes, and I need more. I'm always aware that I have a limited supply, so I have to be careful how I spend it. What's left over is all that I have to do tasks such as form sentences, come up with things to say in a conversation, think during class, walk down a street, or whatever.

I love thinking about hard problems, but I always know that no matter what the hard problem is, while I can do a lot, I won't be able to do as much as possible. I feel as if most people don't have that issue; they can use 100 percent of their mental faculties, and it's not a problem.

I also know that the energy I have available can fluctuate significantly, depending on the environment I'm in. Three people in a room probably won't change it a tremendous amount, but the more people you add and the more complex of an environment, the more energy I have to expend, and the quicker my reserve depletes. You are not going to hear me talking philosophy in a café. I'm not going to have the mental energy available. Some situations are so overwhelming that I have to make choices, such as leaving. I'll know that I only have enough energy to tolerate an environment for thirty minutes, and then I will have to leave, or I will just shut down.

After spending time in an extremely crowded, noisy environment, I might also be a little bit grumpy the next day because I haven't been able to recharge and refill my energy reserves. I don't think that's true in the same way for most people. They don't have to think about what it takes to be themselves or whether they will have the mental energy. But for me, it changes all the time.

I've never been in a truly isolated environment, like solitary confinement in prison, or a place where there was a lot of sensory deprivation, but I have a feeling that it wouldn't work on me. Its intended effect would not happen; instead, I'd have more mental energy to do more things.

LW: What is silence to you?

JORY: I conceptualize silence in terms of things going on, not just sounds. To me, silence means something like meditation or going to a Morning Prayer service in the chapel. Where it's really still, and you're not thinking about stuff. That's what I would consider silence, even if it's not quiet. During those times, there are certainly no noises going on in my head though. That would be terrible.

Most of us who are neurotypical might have what we consider internal monologues with ourselves. We organize our thoughts using words, and we express our internal thoughts with words. But that is not the process that occurs inside Jory's brain.

JORY: There's no language whatsoever connected to my thoughts inside my brain, unless for some reason I have to tell someone else about it. I don't have a "me" voice that says, "On Thursday, you're signed up to help with the chapel and there's dinner afterwards, make sure you don't show up late."

I work with data points. They contain information and look like little beads. I put things in these beads. It could be anything from something I've read in a book to something a professor or a friend has said. Or it could be an observation that I've made— something that was never based in words in the first place. But even if there was language in there at some point, I've removed the language by placing it inside the bead. All the beads are the same, and I treat them all the same. I take whatever knowledge is being processed and put it into Jory format.

That's the first part.

The next is when I want to retrieve something, I get a truck- load of beads out of storage. Their position and location in my mind space are very easily altered. I may make connections, I may not. Sometimes the connections are very arbitrary. Mostly, I just shift the beads around and make a mess of the beads and see what happens. Because while the beads are very tangible to me, the interconnections among them are not. It's all very much done on the fly. And there are no words in there. There's no need for words. Words would just complicate things.

The information I have occupies space; it has some kind of dimensional property. But words aren't like that. To me, the let- ter *A* has no dimensions. I think of words as being like arbitrary streams of light or sets of arbitrary shapes that people have come up with. Whereas with my beads, I've removed all the differentiation among the symbols—there's no *A, B, C, D*. There's none of that confusing extra stuff that language has. Nothing to slow you down or shackle you, none of that ambiguity.

Maybe other people's brains operate like a typewriter, and it's like a stream of words coming in, *bing, bing*. That's how the machine is set up. It's fine, it's not a problem for them. But for me, a stream of words can't exist in bead space or Jory space or whatever you want to call it. It just doesn't work.

LW: How do you organize Jory beads?
JORY: I don't think there's much organization. I think they're easy to fly through really, really quickly when you're searching. I almost feel as if in my laziness, after I've chucked them all over the place, I can search through them really fast. But now that I'm in grad school, I've learned a lot of stuff in the past five years in particular—as anybody who uses their mind actively and enjoys pulling in new information does. Now it seems that because of the amount of information that I have to scan through, it takes a little bit longer. The thing is, I have to scan the whole thing—it's not even organized by areas; rather, when I start thinking about something, my brain does a complete scan. A very tiny fraction of my brain is actively looking at each bead and deciding yes, no, yes, no.

Directly related to energy is the environment. For Jory, some environments are extremely draining and quickly deplete his limited energy resources. We frequently talked about how Jory perceives the world as we experience it—and how that world is not set up to be "hospitable" to autism. At the same time, being able to navigate the external environment is crucial to Jory's ability to function.

JORY: If there's anything that autism has taught me about the environment, it is that you can't escape your environment. You're not a bird. You can't fly away. I suppose on some level you can fly away, but it's a lot more difficult for people to fly away from an individual environment.

Here in England when it's a dark stretch and the sun hasn't poked out for a good many days, people are cranky. The environment has a very pervasive effect. Although, geographers know the dangers of going too far with that, environmental determinism. That was how colonial explorers justified things like slavery and colonialism, by saying that the environment—actually the heat of the sun—was sapping worker productivity and was why Europe was more industrialized. It was basically an intellectual cover for colonialism.

For me at least, the environment is more deterministic than it is for other people. I think my ideal environment is me, but the internal bits. Anywhere there are people, it's going to be hard to find a hospitable environment for autism. That sounds very accusatory, but really, it's nothing against other people. It has nothing to do with anything that other people are doing.

It's very rare when I can reduce my mental expenditure, so it's always invaluable when I can. I mostly do that at home and with people I know really well. When I was going to college, I lived at home, and there was no mental energy expenditure there. At Oxford, especially when we first got here, it took a lot more mental energy, and I was pretty worn out from that process.

A concrete example of how Jory's brain attempts to manage the sensory overload of new or complex environments is illustrated by one anecdote, Jory and the Invisible Window:

JORY: For example, in the house we rented in Oxford, in my room there was a window on the same wall as my bed. And about nine months after we had moved in, Mom and I were talking, and I said there are only skylights in my room, no windows. And she replied, "What are you talking about? There's a window by your bed." And I said, "No, there's not." Well, *there is* a window at the foot of my bed, and I just had not known it was there. All my mind saw was a wall. I think it's because I have a lower-environmental brain level; I'm paying less attention to my environment because I feel like our rental house is my home base. Even though I like to think I have a good amount of mental energy at this point, I still overestimate the amount of mental energy I do have, because I miss something as obvious as a window.

Energy leads us to a conversation about what makes Jory's mind disengage and retreat, literally shut down. (The short answer is people or environments related to people.) Working outward from that point, Jory talks about how he was first able to more fully engage with the outside world.

JORY: In a stressful environment, language and speech would be one of the first things to go. That is because the way I think is not really in terms of language. Closing down communication language-wise actually protects my mind and my ability to think. If I am a castle under siege and the walls are getting thin, pulling up the drawbridge and shutting down communication is how I would protect myself. The need to shut down like this hasn't really happened to me, since I am able to remember things about my life; I feel that very distinctly. But I'm also aware that if I were in an extreme environment and needed to shut down, it would be because I've reached a stage where it's possible my mind will no longer function correctly, and it might not be fully recoverable. Not only could I no longer process what's on the outside, but what's inside would be damaged as well.

Interestingly, what makes me want to shut down or come very close is anything related to people. I can stand next to a waterfall, a noisy nature environment with a similar decibel level to a shopping mall, and the effect would be very different. I'd be fine by the waterfall and miserable in the mall. Which is strange because if you think about it, it's the same decibel level and it also involves a lot of sensory stimuli. But there's a distinction: the mall involves other people and the stimuli comes from people. It's even different with other living things. When my pet bird Federer screeches really loudly, that can sort of impair my thinking. But not to the same extent as people or people-related noise, such as cars, city noise, just the sounds of people moving. Especially people I don't know. Most people can somehow subconsciously auto—tune out noise. I'm not able to do that. I have to do it actively and that takes effort. It's fine, especially if I want to be there, but it does drain energy. And for years, I couldn't do it.

But I know I have to be out of my ideal environment. Probably when I was a teenager and Mom was encouraging me to be in places I didn't want to be, I learned that I can be anywhere, if I have some tools to be there and am okay with being there.

Now there are events I want to go to, and I will expend the mental energy to do those things. I enjoy movies and plays. A harder place is something like a bar. I personally don't really drink. The only reason I would go is because someone else I know is going. I try to be aware of making the effort with Mom, for instance, because Mom likes doing things that I do not. But sometimes I say, "Why don't we do this instead?" Which I can do with Mom, but not with a larger group.

Talking about Memories,
Both Missing Them and Making Them:

Much of Jory's early life is a blank. He existed in a kind of void, struggling to communicate, struggling to process and make sense of the world around him. He has almost no memories of that time. Only the briefest flashes of images and experiences are preserved in his mind.

JORY: The very first thing I can remember is a rocking horse that I did not like. I don't know when we had the rocking horse. It might have been when we lived in Kentucky or Indiana. I have no idea why I have this memory, except that I used to have a nightmare about the rocking horse, and I was definitely a little afraid of the rocking horse. From Indiana, I also remember getting stuck in the snow in the front yard one time. It snowed really badly—we were at the end of a cul-de-sac and my brothers built a snow slide. I can't remember if I was using the slide or was just in the snow, but I fell down. It freaked me out because the snow was deep, I couldn't see, and I didn't know where I was. I remember a few other things from Indiana, but they're very sporadic. I vaguely remember watching Barney on television and I vaguely remember what Mom looked like at that time. I think my little sister ran into the corner of a piece of furniture, but I'm not sure if that was in Indiana or after we moved to South Carolina. Very few of my memories have any physicality. Like the cold day and the snow, I wouldn't remember the feeling of cold. The memories are also all random, and mostly either objects or events or environments, rather than people.

I generally remember the move to South Carolina. By remember, I mean I specifically remember one instance from moving in where the living room in our house had wood floors and was the largest room and was very empty. I had my *Blue's Clues* blanket. And I remember my friend James was there that day, but I don't remember specifically meeting him.

The reason why it is difficult for me to remember has less to do with language and my lack of being able to communicate than with the fact that I was beneath the surface—if you are the one beneath the surface, you don't have much opportunity to observe and create memories. Perhaps why I remember the rocking horse and almost nothing else in the room—because it's almost nonsensical that I could remember this specific thing in such seemingly high detail, but nothing else—is that for some reason I had a glimpse through the surface and that was one of the few things I observed.

LW: When do you feel like you more consistently breached the surface? What changed?

JORY: From my understanding of all the stories I've heard, I was not good in any way at communicating anything. What I've been told is that my reactions to things bothering me in the environment were often very visceral. I had a lot of tantrums, a lot of screaming; I did not cope very well. It was that I couldn't express myself, but it was also that it wasn't fully me there in the first place—I feel like it doesn't make sense to say "uncommunicative" because it wasn't me. Then, there was a period where I was stronger, if you will, still beneath the surface, but like barely.

Somewhere around age seven or eight, there's more, but it's still blurry. It was a gradual process until I was more in control, until there was more of a balance between me and autism. There were still times where I couldn't fully maintain that equilibrium, and I would still react to the environment. Not until at least when I was a mid-teenager was I at least nominally in control most of the time.

LW: What were environments that you tolerated and environments that you just wanted to escape from?

JORY: One thing that Mom and I would do most evenings after we moved to South Carolina is watch the nightly news and then *Wheel of Fortune* and *Jeopardy!* I really enjoyed that. I always liked spending time with Mom, but spending time in a really autistic way. I never wanted to be more than a couple of feet from Mom. If she left, I would go crazy. I don't remember this, but I know from other accounts that I would go crazy if she left to go to the grocery store or whatever.

I remember very little about school before I was home-schooled, starting in second grade. I do remember leaving for the bus, which I did not like, because it meant I had to leave the house and Mom. I remember just waiting for the bus in the front room in the chair watching out the window with Mom. Bad times. But other than that, I don't remember too much from the school itself or what I did at the school.

I have a limited subset of things that I know about myself. But it's curious to me because I can't really necessarily say with any confidence that this bit is mine and that bit is from sort of shared family knowledge. An example is I was very attached to Mom and was always very upset when she would leave, even if I was left with my older brother Tyler or somebody else I really liked and trusted. I have some recollection of what that felt like, but I've also been told a lot about my reactions to that as well. So the extent to which I'm remembering my own reactions versus somebody else telling me what my reaction was at the time is unclear to me.

I know through a combination of limited memory plus shared knowledge that I made a transition from being upset when Mom left—standing by the door and refusing to do anything until she came back—to being upset when Mom left but then hanging out with Tyler, and getting really excited when she came back. Eventually I moved on to I'm okay with Mom leaving for short periods of time and not getting upset about it, and then I was fine with her coming in and out at any time.

I don't really remember what it felt like. I remember the sense that something was wrong about this situation. The environment went from stable to unstable, and it would be that way until Mom came back. I feel like I was hyperaware of what was missing in the home environment. Mom was the centerpiece of that environment. When Mom left, it was upsetting, not just because I missed Mom and my attachment to Mom, but because the home environment was, to my mind, no longer in a stable state without her. It didn't matter why she was gone or how long, it was as if the middle had been removed, and I didn't have anything else to put in the middle, so I just stared at the door until the middle came back.

One of the favorite family stories is how I would throw a tantrum anytime I was in a car and the sunlight filtered through the window and touched me. One time, we were driving from Indiana, I think, to Florida. They tried to cover up all the windows so no sun would enter the vehicle. But inevitably a ray slipped through, and I would start screaming. It wasn't a fun car ride, but they didn't turn the car around; they kept going to our destination.

I have absolutely zero recollection of the whole incident. My family usually retells the story in a group at a restaurant, and it's always a contrast because I have usually been in a car about fifteen minutes earlier, when it was sunny out, and I was fine. It's just interesting to think, Oh, yeah, that was me, and I don't remember, which is great for me because apparently it wouldn't have been a good memory.

Another place that was terrible for me was the mall. I was going to have a tantrum no matter what happened. I did not have any fun at the mall, and it was a lot to process. I do have some recollection of going to the mall with my mom and little sister, Lauren, for back-to-school clothes shopping. I had the most trouble in the corners with crowds; I had difficulty concentrating and hearing if Mom was trying to tell me something.

But I'm not particularly interested in how I behaved in my

childhood versus now unless somebody wants to know. It's not like I think about how much have I progressed or how has autism changed for me as an experience in my day-to-day life up to now. It's just not something I think about at all.

LW: What do you think helped you to start processing and saving memories?

JORY: Age eleven or twelve would be the earliest I start to get more concrete memories as opposed to things that happened in high frequency or very random specific instances, like that rocking horse. I remember particular activities that were done in repetition; they stood out. It also helped when I was in an environment where there were almost no other stressors or new stimuli.

I always had home school in the breakfast room right outside the kitchen. It was the exact same routine every day, the same chair, the same table, the books were exactly where I had left them the day before. There was an absurd level of consistency. That was helpful; it was all in balance.

There was a window overlooking the bird feeder. To start the school day, I would see if there were any birds out, watch for birds, and count birds for a few minutes. I remember the order that school typically went. Phonics was typically first, followed by math. I hated both of those. But I liked order of events, or the fact that I would often take little breaks and watch birds. I remember hanging out with James, playing video games in our upstairs living room or going outside on the driveway and riding scooters. The memory of it is not specific, as in, Oh, I remember exactly what James looked like in that instance. It's just general. Not until much later, when I was a teenager, did I have a more or less uninterrupted sequence of events. If you were to ask me about an event from college, I might need some prompting if it wasn't significant, but I probably would recall details about the event, as opposed to the period when I was homeschooled, which has a very low probability of any specific event coming out.

For instance, when I was younger, I apparently had a train game and I would make a road like a train track. I would set up all the little pieces in a very specific way and would get mad if anybody moved them. Everyone else in my family remembers it, but for me it is just not there. I have no memory of said game. I have no memory of getting mad about its being moved. No memory of the room where I played that game, because I always played it in the same spot. It's like a gaping hole, and most of my memories are like that.

Sometimes things from childhood will come up. Someone will ask, "Don't you know this?" And it will be a childhood playground rhyme that everybody else knows. I have to say, "I don't know that rhyme." I don't know the games that kids do with their hands, like patty-cake. It's interesting because childhood is a really important thing for people, very positive in many cases. But the fact that I have massive holes doesn't make what I do remember less positive.

Birds and Video Games

LW: What are the connections between birds and video games?
JORY: For me, video games are like somebody's crafted a world that you get to be an active participant in. The games

give you a sense of freedom because you don't really know what's going to come next. Birds are even more unpredictable. They exist in a world, but they are independent actors, and they do a lot of unexpected things. When you are observing a bird, you feel almost like a participant in its world. When you see a twitch of its head, you wonder, "Is he looking for food, or did he spy a friend in a tree or a predator?" You can both feel connected to the bird's sense of freedom, of being able to just fly off, and also get that connection to the narrative and the interaction that that bird is having in a place that you can observe but are still separate from.

It's similar with video games. You're interacting with a world—it's a little bit more directly crafted, but you're still interacting with a world—and you can think what you like about that story, but the story has the capacity to surprise you and to take you in a new direction. Both are also visually appealing. A video game has artists to make the world come alive and be magical or mysterious or however they want to design it, and birds are visually appealing as well. Even the drab birds are visually appealing and interesting because evolutionarily speaking, they're drab so they don't get eaten. There's always beauty, even if it's just various shades of a neutral tone.

4

Emotional Distancing

Talking about Emotions:

One of the major stereotypes about autism is that people on the autistic spectrum lack emotions. But, interestingly, our own scientific understanding of human emotion is in the midst of a major revision.

New neuroscience research is centered around the concept that emotions are not intrinsic to human beings—that they are not hardwired as part of our collective makeup—but instead are individually constructed by the receiver's brain, using physical, mental, and even cultural cues. Rather than being universal, each person's emotional makeup is both subjective and slightly different.

Psychologist and neuroscience researcher Lisa Feldman Barrett makes the case that a central way the brain creates emotions is by making predictions. It separates input based on similarities and differences and then summarizes that information to create concepts, such as happy or sad.

Jory's experiences with emotion and his understanding of

emotion are both very individual and very complex. He does not, for example, experience "hurt feelings" and emotional wounds. Large-group displays of emotion make him uneasy, in much the same way that he gets uneasy around people drinking alcohol, because after a few drinks the personalities and language of the people who are drinking noticeably shift, and they give off different signals.

We had many discussions about the multiple facets and nuances of emotion, but within those, one statement stands out: When he said, "Emotions seem to be happening further away from me."

It is not that Jory lacks emotions, but rather that he has his own individual emotional register.

JORY: I can't inhabit someone else's mind, but from what I understand, I'm pretty sure my emotions are the same or at least very similar. My response is probably the difference. I am affected less. Not in the sense that I'm not aware of emotions, but I can basically ignore them for all intents and purposes. Even positive emotions, I'll sort of be aware of, but not fully internalize in the same way. For me, there's also no such thing as being a little bit sad or slightly happy. I either am or I'm not. It has to reach a certain threshold of intensity.

I have to think about everything connected with emotions. It's almost like there is a sensory experience, and to process it, I have to conduct a rapid large-scale analysis. I feel like whenever I do have an emotional reaction, it's always specific in the sense that I can tell you what caused its formation. It doesn't just appear. It's almost like a chemical reaction, where with most people it would just happen automatically. But there's an extra step that I have to go through before that sort of process can happen.

I also don't usually hold on to emotions. Sad, happy, upset, joyful, those are all things where I understand the definition and have been aware of that emotion before. But I normally don't keep the emotion around or reflect on it.

I feel like I have a different mental positioning for emotions, not necessarily looking down on them from above, but maybe pushing them off to the side. Emotions seem to be happening further away from me. If I do nothing, then whatever emotion it is will just stream past and then it will be gone.

I would describe it as if you're walking somewhere, you're moving in a straight line, and out of the corner of your eye, somebody sort of says something and you're not sure if it's entirely directed at you, but you think it is. Depending on the situation, you either keep going and ignore it, or turn and look. Or you catch a glimpse of something out of the corner of your eye. If it's a lot to process in your visual field, you're going to ignore what's in the corner, versus sometimes you may take a quick look. But then you move your eyes forward again.

It's not that an emotion is less important, but it's less immediate. Even really strong emotional specks take up a little more than a corner, but never so much that you can't see the rest.

Similar to how Jory finds reading facial expressions and body language during conversations to be challenging, he has difficulties picking up on other people's emotions and understanding them, regardless of how they are expressed.

But his efforts to recognize emotion have led him to make some very interesting observations about the ways that crowds embrace a common emotion. He is deeply curious how so many people can end up in "emotional sync" and what underlies that process. For example, do people in a crowd consciously choose to be angry together, or is it more of a subconscious, instinctive process, where everyone joins in almost without thinking?

JORY: I'm generally bad at noticing and reading other people's reactions. There are a few emotions that I catch really quickly, and those are usually the negative ones. When somebody's hurt, angry or when they're fearful, those display really rapid responses in people's behavioral shifts. All the other ones are slow enough where it's not quite as stark.

I am aware of when large groups of people all feel the same thing quickly. It's weird because I can feel that something has changed, like people weren't angry before but now they're angry. I personally am not angry at all, but I can sense that now everybody else is angry, and that's really weird. What happened between ten seconds ago and now? In some cases, I was not able to witness what happened. Maybe it was something that happened at the other end of the crowd, but now everyone's angry, because it's a crowd. That is very interesting to me.

One time I attended a big protest at Oxford. I popped in to see what was "going on." There were a few counterprotesters along with the protesters in the crowd. But it was very weird to me, because even though both sides were supposedly opposed, what I perceived was that they were all feeling the same things. They were all still connected in that way. It did kind of freak me out, it was odd.

LW: Odd how?

JORY: Because where does this feeling come from? And where did it start? Did it start with one person? Did it start with a general knowledge that just sort of became emotional among everyone at the same time? Did people consciously accept that? Did people say, "I'm going to be angry now because I want to be angry," or was it subconscious? Did they have any agency in becoming angry? Could they not have become angry if they had sufficient wherewithal? It's a very interesting question to me as to whether you can resist a crowd in that way. I don't know.

I didn't stay long because it wasn't a safe place for Daisy. Especially in the inner bits, she got kind of squeezed a little bit. But there were a couple of instances where some person was really angry and then they realized they had almost stepped on my dog's foot. They stopped to say, "Oh, I'm really sorry," and they broke out of it. But then they reentered that emotion. It was such a stark contrast. I could see it in their eyes in particular. Being able to go in and out of emotions like that—it's just very, very odd to me. Any sort of decrease in the ability to be separate and more in control is concerning. I've been to some protests and find them really good displays of democracy in many cases, but it does freak me out, even if I find it to be a useful civic engagement practice.

LW: What's the most disconcerting part for you about that type of behavior?

JORY: What I find hard to comprehend is do people have a set of rules for governing that behavior, or do they just latch on to a feeling in air? When it's that strong, I can also sort of feel it. And

I really don't like that feeling. I do not like it when crowds start to act in a coordinated fashion. To me, it's like all the individuals have become lost in some way, but then they can come back. So it's not like a permanent loss, but to me it does feel like a loss, maybe because in part I can't join in myself. I could be present in a crowd, but I can't really latch on in that way. And I wouldn't want to do that either.

I also get this uneasy feeling when people are drinking alcohol because I notice that their behavior shifts, their language shifts, and the signals that they give off shift as well. I have real trouble dealing with shifts in signals. When people join a crowd's emotion, suddenly they go from displaying different signals to displaying really similar signals, really quickly. That's probably what's disconcerting to me. In the same way, when one individual person has had a few drinks, it changes their signals, even if they're not totally drunk. That makes me uneasy as well.

Jory does not experience "hurt feelings" in the traditional way most neurotypical people do. He discusses what happens when other people make cutting or hurtful remarks to him and his responses.

JORY: What stops someone with autism, like me, is stimuli—the number of people, noise, lighting and so on. But if somebody tries to stop me from doing something by hurting my feelings or making me feel bad, I keep powering through. It's not because I feel those hurts and then ignore them or shunt them away or overcome them. They are just not there.

During one class at Oxford, we discussed energy conservation. I made a comment about considering the equity issues of an energy tax, because I'm very conscious of how much energy all my medical devices use, and another student responded with a comment that was apparently too dismissive of me for other people in the class. The next week, I got a lot of comments like "Oh, are you doing okay?" and I had no idea what they were referencing. It never registered with me as a problem.

When I was in college, an animal rights guy came up to me and said service dogs are a form of animal cruelty, that my dog shouldn't be a slave to anyone. Something quite insensitive and implying that Daisy's unhappy, and she clearly would be much happier if I left her at home. I was going to talk to him, but he left in a hurry. He wasn't interested in an actual conversation. What I was going to say was "Oh, that's an incorrect statement. She's happy, and she would be super pissed if I left her at home."

I think a lot of people standing around me were horrified at his comments. I just kept walking to class, but to them it looked like I must be really devastated and was running away. But for me, that wasn't the case. To me, it was simply a quick thought: Oh, that was a very rude thing to say. I wouldn't have even responded to the insult or the derogatory part. It had no effect. It's not because I didn't think it was important, but it wasn't important to me.

If that incident with Daisy happened today, I would probably respond, "That's not acceptable to say to someone who's disabled, and while I don't care about it, you should not say that to other people who are not me but have a service dog. It would probably ruin their week." Especially considering the tone and the manner in which it was delivered, both of which are things that I came to understand later, after talking with other people. Because while it may not affect me, I know it could be really shattering for someone else.

For me, that shattering never happens, and it never would happen, which sounds really cold, but it's made me realize that the emotional bit that I'm missing is very important to everybody else.

I've had instances where friends have said to me, "I'm so sorry such and such happened. Are you feeling okay?" My response is, "What are you talking about?" I had no idea, I was like, Why are you comforting me? I also think people conflate comforting or responding to a bad situation with only providing an emotional response, sort of a big bear hug is going to fix this. In my case, it's confusing. An emotional response, a physical hug, those types of things are not going to help me. They are simply more unfamiliar things to process.

LW: Do you view emotions as a negative or a positive?
JORY: There are benefits to not being easily influenced by emotion. I think my life would be horrible if I was able to be wounded by emotion. The fact that people can get backstabbed or have emotional confrontations seems to add a whole new horrible dimension. I don't have to deal with that, I'm just observing it.

I wonder if anybody's ever thought, "What if emotions were just something you could sample, the way you sample food from the grocery market?" I know there are very positive things that can happen with emotion. I'll never know that in the same way. But I'll never be at risk of nefarious things happening to me in the same way that other people are.

LW: So how would you describe your emotional register?

JORY: People have said that I don't display emotions the way that other people tend to. For instance, like most other people, I get nervous from public speaking. Not only do people not notice that, they actually think that I'm weirdly calm. When I was preparing for my Rhodes interview, I called the director of the Truman Foundation, who was in my interview for the Truman Scholars, which was the most nerve-racking thing I had done in my life. I thought I figuratively face-planted in the interview. I told him I was hoping to be less nervous for my Rhodes interview and what would he recommend?

He told me how oddly calm and unflappable I appeared, and that was when I realized, Wow, people say I'm a good or a decent public speaker because they can't see what I may actually be feeling or sensing, which is very interesting. I don't display very well, which I find hilarious. Because of course, I have that problem with other people, not being able to see what they display, so it gives me some small satisfaction that at least I return the favor.

Beyond being nervous, I get frustrated sometimes, but it's a very unemotional emotion. For me, it's an intellectual recognition that something is wrong, and I don't know how to fix it. Often nobody else recognizes it as wrong. The assumption or the activity is not going to be modified to make it comfortable for me; instead, I have to listen or participate regardless.

But I think it is helpful to have somebody to talk to. I appreciate being able to share my frustrations, and I appreciate that Mom is willing to listen to me. I try to do that for other people. In that sense, I enjoy communicating with people about things on my mind or things I'm concerned about.

I always try to be aware of and not to say anything about identity-related issues. I don't know how to process that kind of information. I consider that ironic to some extent because my position with having autism and other disabilities is at least partly similar to what a minority group might feel when they talk about needing things like safe spaces. Because no human-generated space is going to be a safe space for me forever.

But this is so complex and nuanced, I know I'd get it wrong, so I tend to not speak about it unless I'm having a one-on-one conversation where I can know there's some trust, and the person will know that whatever I was trying to get across was not meant to harm.

LW: Tell me about your frustrations. What frustrates you?

JORY: Over the past two years I've studied and learned a lot about climate change from many different perspectives. My own thinking about climate change has become much more nuanced, but as I have spent more and more time studying the issue, it has also left me frustrated. My personal conclusion is that there is some widespread, problematic thinking going on, which could benefit from a more autistic approach.

For example, imagine a small town by a river. Then someone comes and opens an industrial plant. They seem quite friendly, but a few years after they arrived, the river turns orange from the pollutants they have dumped into it. All the fish die, and people get sick from the river water. They make the plant change its practices or pay to clean up the river, or maybe everyone agrees a different type of plant would probably work better. But the central point is that everyone agrees that this harm to the river is ideally not acceptable. I see climate change in an identical way, just the spatial scale and the system complexity are higher.

What I struggle with is wondering why people have different responses to climate change than to horrible local pollution. Why does the same logic vanish when we stop discussing a river and start discussing the planet? To my mind, there must be an error in their thinking process. Perhaps they are allowing emotions or rhetoric to corrupt their reasoning. Or perhaps they are thinking linearly and can't make the right connections with their version of thinking beads? I find that frustrating because the way I think results in a different view, and it is difficult for me to understand why there is such a difference—or any difference at all—when the issue is objectively observable to everyone. You would think that the response to dumping pollutants into a fluid would not change arbitrarily based on things like emotion, politics, or money, which from my perspective are not actual objective data points, but rather things that tend to corrupt data.

JORY: On a personal level, I got slightly more frustrated in England than I did at the University of South Carolina, but that's usually because something that doesn't frustrate other people frustrates me a lot. When you have too many frustrations stack up, it's just really irritating. I was struck how at Oxford, someone will come and speak to a group. They will start off talking about us being future government ministers or business leaders, and that assumption will irritate me. Nobody else will notice.

But the fact that the speaker assumed multiple people in the room are going to be running things just because they are here is irritating to me. From my perspective, there's actually no objective reason for this. It's not because of increased knowledge or increased experience or wisdom from simply being here. Instead, it has everything to do with the assumptions that go into having an Oxford degree, assumptions that everybody thinks are real, but I don't.

I recognize the effect of a degree, but I also think if people stopped making a big deal about it, its power would largely vanish. Maybe it's a weird privilege of autism to have things like that be unimportant. I find those assumptions irritating, but I think that's okay as long as I don't spread my irritations to everybody within earshot because I believe they need to think the same way.

Sometimes people that don't know me particularly well assume I have interests in things based on what I have done. Such as because I went to Oxford, they think I might be interested in money or power. And that's not true at all. But if most people asked, I wouldn't even bother sharing my view because I feel like they would be too likely to get the wrong impression of why I think that.

For me, Oxford is not about a degree, but about the place, the people, and the journey. The ancient and timeless libraries, quiet walks in the gardens, learning to sing, and Scottish dancing, the people I grew to love in chapel. My experience was so rich. Oxford has a deeper meaning than any credential and represents a time in my life that I'll be forever grateful to have experienced.

LW: How do you handle emotions yourself? What provokes an emotional response in you? What is your response to your own emotions?

JORY: I do still have feelings and emotions, but my response to them is what's different, I guess. My ability in most cases to shut them off is weird to people. But there are a few instances where

I have a strong emotion, and I just have to be neutral and ignore it and it will go away.

What causes these emotions tends to be broadscale, like structural racism or poverty or bad things that have happened. They will give me a kind of sad feeling, but I don't accept it because that's not productive. I think it's advantageous to be hopeful in all instances.

When I feel a particularly strong emotion, it's almost like redirecting lightning. Lots of times you can redirect the lightning just fine but other times you need to switch to lightning rod mode and make it become meaningless.

I also do have thoughts that are meaningful as apart from logical thoughts, but I don't know if I would call them emotions. If I remember something that's meaningful to me, it will be more of a variety of factors, and maybe the emotions are kind of an aside. If you think of a play, for other people, emotions might be the whole set: the way the backdrop and the curtains and the props are all used to set the scene. For me, an emotion might be one minor actor in a group on the stage for one scene.

LW: What are your responses to specific emotions, such as anger, sadness, or happiness?

JORY: I think anger can sometimes be acceptable, but not productive. I struggle to think of any instances of where anger is productive. In that sense, it makes it very easy to reject. I intellectually have reasons for rejecting it, so the analytic portion of my brain helps with the shunting. Whereas with sadness, I feel like the intellectual side of my brain is not helping. The fact that certain bad things in society exist is sad, and that's acceptable much more than anger is. But because it's an emotion, I still remove it. Even happy emotions, I sort of observe them. I don't shunt them away actively or lightning rod them away, but I still can't be affected by them too much. I let them float around over there and observe them like a nice flower. It's not as if I'm completely unemotional—sometimes I am affected by emotions, but they have to be incredibly strong.

Not Feeling Stress and Not Processing Fear:

For many years, neuroscientists believed that the fear response in humans and animals was concentrated in the amygdala, a structure in the lower reaches of the brain, not far from the brain stem. But some of the latest brain research calls into question that relationship.

"The brain must have multiple ways of creating fear, and therefore the emotion category 'Fear' cannot be necessarily localized to a specific region," notes Lisa Feldman Barrett in her book How Emotions Are Made: The Secret Life of the Brain. *Instead, she argues that the brain contains "core systems," which are capable of "creating a wide variety of mental states." She describes our brain neurons as being "multipurpose," rather than each one having a dedicated, single use.*

For his part, Jory links stress and fear together as one related unit. Although, he describes himself as being both low stress and low fear. And he "rejects" highly emotional responses to either.

JORY: What causes me to feel stress, such as social interactions, tends to be very different from what causes stress in other people. Some people even find it weird because situations where other people think I should have stress, I don't. I can't remember the last time I was stressed about anything academic. It's not that I don't care about the outcome, but I guess my perspective is a little different. I don't think that worrying would be helpful anyway. Toward the end of college, I kept a 4.0, but I didn't do it super intentionally, I focused on learning and didn't stress about exams. If I got a B in biology, it wouldn't have wrecked my day. Whereas, I think for some people, it would have.

I don't have much fear either. Some people might be concerned about death, whereas for me that's completely irrelevant because I have the perspective of well, statistically speaking, either of us could have a heart attack at any moment and that's just the way it is, right? There's nothing you can do about it. I'd be fine getting any number of corporeal diseases which led to my death except for maybe Alzheimer's or anything that leads to general amnesia or loss of memory. I wouldn't enjoy that.

One external thing I don't like is horror movies, I don't watch them. A media thing that's specifically programmed to prey on your biology I am indeed susceptible to. But in real life, I don't think I'm afraid of much. If I were to see the absolute biggest spider I've ever seen in my life crawl out of the pipe behind the computer, I am aware of the response where your heart rate noticeably picks up. But there's no emotion attached to it. I would struggle to think of a reason why fear would be appropriate. If I did encounter a situation that would be considered "fearful," I would certainly recognize the potential for negative outcomes probably just as rapidly as anybody else. But my personal response is not going to be bettered in a way by an emotional response.

Here, I think the spider example is a good one. In some way, the emotional response is automatic. I can't prevent my heart rate from going up. But I can choose to not go running and screaming out of the house. Because that would not be a helpful solution to the problem. The first response is automatic, but the second one is technically under my control or your control, even if most people don't exercise that control.

One thing I am worried about or strongly concerned about emotionally is losing access to part of my brain or at least losing the ability to keep control of my brain. But that's paired with an extreme lack of concern about my inability to control the outside world. If I was riding in a plane that was going to crash, I would just do the logical thing in the air, and I wouldn't be concerned at all. I certainly would not be panicking on the way down because that's not helpful. It absolutely has no use or relevance whatsoever; it's just an emotional reaction, which I wouldn't have.

For example, I don't have an emotional response to climate change, but I am concerned about the harm from a lack of action on climate change. But I think about it in the sense of, Wow, wouldn't it be the dumbest thing ever if one of the smartest species on the planet did nothing because of emotion or politics or something else and we caused our own extinction? I think about those things, but not all the time, and I don't have any issues about letting it go until the next time I think about it.

There's always been this part of my brain where I'll put information that's not appealing to my brain. Or things come in that are sometimes not processed; they're rejected. It's not really a conscious preference; it might just be the way my mind works. I have to take in a lot on a regular basis, so my brain can't accept all of it. I don't hold on to things that someone else might consider frightening or upsetting or distressing. I don't do too much with anything like that.

Emoticons:

I really don't read too much into them, to be honest. If somebody sends a happy face, whatever, that's fine. Or if somebody sends a funny face, I'll be like, Oh, that's a funny face. I think they're kind of funny. But if you try to encode substance and then string multiples of them together, I can't really get that. If people want to make a language out of it, all the power to them. I will not be joining them on their quest.

A View of Jory's Preferred Comfort Zone

Hopefully, I'm going to work to help solve social or environmental problems. Those definitely affect people, and that's the main reason why I'm interested in them. But it's not emotional in the sense that I don't know these people. These problems impact how people feel, but I don't think the response has to be emotional. That doesn't mean that I still can't have provided some very unemotional assistance in the sense of fixing one of their problems. But if I solved somebody's problem for them, and then they came up and gave me a hug later? I'd rather they not.

LW: Do you cry?

JORY: Sometimes. *Marley and Me*, the movie about the dog, got me pretty good. That was rough. And there've been a couple of other movies like that. The major point driving the theme is sad. My sister was very proud that I shed a couple of tears at the end of the musical *Hamilton* in London. I feel like the last time I had more than one or two tears was at the end of senior year of college when I was compiling photo albums. There was one that I put together for Cocky's Reading Express, which did get to me a little bit. I also cried at the last service I attended in the Worcester College Chapel. I spent a lot of time there over the past two years.

Moments where I reflected on a journey or the end of a really meaningful experience, those experiences tend to be of an emotional quality. Sometimes I will get sad about the state of world affairs or the state of the environment. But it's usually an abstract concept, so I won't cry over it; I'll think about it on an intellectual level.

Some other weird things always reach out to me. Like a teddy bear being left alone, that always gets to me. The movies where the teddy bear is left behind because the kid grows up. That gets me every time. Weirdly specific things like that, but it's not a regular occurrence, for sure. Otherwise I have what I call "zooming out moments" where something will happen in the environment, or someone will say something, that will just get me to think of a lot of things simultaneously.

LW: How about happiness? What is your view of happiness? How do you experience it—how does it feel to you?

JORY: Happiness is pretty vague, isn't it? I feel like I am a cheerful person, because optimism is more logical than pessimism, so you may as well just choose that. I also think of happiness sometimes as contentedness or as gratitude. There are definitely times when I am or am not content or grateful. One thing I notice is that I can't conceptualize a single concept of happiness. The pieces of camaraderie with friends, contentedness, cheerfulness, optimism—most people smush all those together into one big emotional term called happy, and I can't do that. I have to split it. All the components are still there, but I can only talk about them as pieces, because they make more sense when they're concrete. I can tie them to things in the world or experiences in a way that I can't with emotion.

Sad, I feel like, has fewer components. Sad also has to do with negativity in the environment. For some reason optimism/hope has left the system—hopefully for a temporary amount of time. You can be sad and in no way have had something bad happen to you or have lost your hope in humanity.

Talking about Other People's Emotions:

Jory is extremely conscious of his own struggles with emotional awareness and responses.

He is deeply concerned about inadvertently hurting someone else or causing pain because he has not picked up on their words or non-

verbal signals and thus has not responded appropriately. He worries
about and tries to watch every word that he speaks. And this from a
young man who at the start of his life could hardly speak at all.

Listening to him, I was repeatedly struck by the deep burden
and responsibility he feels to not injure other people's emotional
well-being. Jory's various references to his own inadequacies—"I'm
bad at"—made me want to interrupt him to apologize for every-
one who has ever made him feel that he is somehow a lesser person
or has forced upon him a custodial role for other people's feelings.

On his own, Jory has developed a very unique way to compen-
sate for some of his emotional intelligence shortcomings. He read
a manual that most people would probably largely ignore. As he
says, "Who knows how much of the world's knowledge is locked up
in manuals that nobody's thought to read?"

LW: Pull out some Jory beads and give me a picture of how you
envision other people's emotions, how they appear to you, and
how you pick up on them.

JORY: I don't think emotions are always linked to fragility; they
can sometimes be linked to strength. I'd envision it like walking
down a sidewalk where most of it is pavement. But occasionally
there are some eggshells and rocks that are the same color as
the pavement. If you step on the rocks, you think, Ow, but that's
because of somebody's emotional strength that you are not expecting. And if you step on the eggshells, they break. I like that
image because if I'm looking at the sidewalk, it can be difficult, if
the rocks and the eggshells are the same color, to pick out which
one is where as I walk.

A more explicit emotion is easier for me to pick up on than

implicit emotion. If somebody is feeling down or anxious or something like that, they may say something which most people would pick up on. But if they did not literally say "I'm feeling anxious," I might not pick up on that feeling. Or I would misinterpret it. If someone who is super stressed-out studying for exams says, "I haven't been sleeping well," I may not connect it. If I'm reminded that it's exam period, then I'll be like oh, they were feeling anxious and that's why they couldn't sleep.

Most people don't explicitly display anxiety, or if they do, it's really subtle. I was having breakfast with a music major, and he had a recital later in the day. Toward the end of our conversation, he mentioned that he was feeling nervous about the day ahead. Once he said that explicitly, it made me connect other things that I hadn't picked up on before but were now more easily noticeable, like he was drinking copious amounts of water. I saw that, and I just thought he was really thirsty. But I didn't really pick up on the fact that he's nervous so that's why he's drinking so much water. I would not have thought anything of it until it was explicitly pointed out that he was in an emotional state.

LW: What are some of the most difficult things for you in terms of handling other people's emotions?

JORY: The things I struggle with the most are either I didn't respond to something because I didn't fully know what was going on or something I said that was misinterpreted and made someone feel badly or hurt. People are good at hiding when they're hurt or feeling bad. That's the area where I'm most at risk.

Even something as simple as when a person makes a comment that gets me thinking, and I'll race ten steps ahead, and I may draw a different conclusion from them. I still have to remind myself not to jump ahead to my answer, because that's generally very demeaning and dismissive. I do understand that if everybody operated like me, nobody would be hurt emotionally, but I'm fine with the fact that people are.

And in some sense, it's understandable that if you are impacted by emotions, then language is very important. When someone stops you from speaking, when somebody stops your language, that means something to you. Whereas for me, language means absolutely nothing. I have to watch out for stuff like that.

One of the most difficult things for Jory to manage is other people's purely emotional responses, especially their intensely visceral reactions.

JORY: Visceral reactions are also difficult for me because, whether or not they are justified, I never see them as helpful in terms of getting your goal achieved.

I have to remind myself of two things. One, if this person is having that strong of a reaction, they literally can't think of anything else. It's not the time to suggest anything else.

And then two, I have to remind myself that I can contribute. I usually don't contribute unless requested or I can think of something that would be helpful. I have to think really hard so that I don't say just anything that I'm thinking. Instead, it needs to be a nice generality that might be helpful to hear. Like acknowledging that their reaction comes from a place of meaning, no matter how hard that is for me, because my logical sense is this emotional reaction is clearly not helpful for you, and possibly in a day's time, you would agree with me. But I still have to acknowledge it and recognize that it comes from a place of meaning and then sort of decide what to do there.

LW: That type of response is very sophisticated and self-aware. How did you learn to do this?

JORY: I'm very much aware that I have no idea what's going on, and almost anything I think is going to be unhelpful. I do tend to recognize that pretty quickly, or I'll make one mistake and pick up on the mistake right away. In the past, my reaction had been pretty much nothing because I wasn't sure what to do. But I think other people often have unhealthy reactions, and they totally know what's going on. So I have that excuse.

But there was a particular experience that really helped me. It was signing up to be a peer leader for the University of South Carolina's first-year seminar. All the peer leaders had to take a class on how to facilitate conversations, and we were given a manual. There was a section in the manual on how to respond to people that are in distress or emotional. It was very specific, step-by-step. I loved it.

Step one was acknowledge their concern and discuss—help the participant discover where it comes from and then make sure you help find organic solutions. Make sure you don't use these words [the manual provided a specific list of words], which imply judgment. Instead, use these words, which are neutral and add more explanation. It listed phrases you could use, which was not unknown material to me, but it was very much like, Oh, thank God, somebody provided me with a manual.

I saved that manual. I still have it as a file on my computer.

And every now and again when I don't have anything to do, I will sometimes look at it because it's super helpful. It's stuff like when you respond to somebody's contribution, make sure you say thank you for saying that, which is neutral and welcoming, as opposed to responding with anything like a judgment or an imperative type question. It gave the reasons why responding that way is not going to be helpful and not going to help somebody grow. It had a metaphor that used a plant: the way you help a plant grow is by giving it what it needs, not what the gardener thinks is best. It was mind-blowing to me to have that level of specificity and say do this, not that. It's almost like now I have a "be a good friend" mode that I can activate.

It's a weird paradox: that being completely unaware and knowing I was completely unaware made me realize what I couldn't do. So when I was told things, I would be receptive. Now I make sure that I think about my response before I say it. I make sure that it first acknowledges and then welcomes the contribution, where it's coming from, acknowledging all of that before proceeding. Following that kind of rule. It's simple, but, yes, it's very hard to do. You have to be self-aware. Some people might call it high emotional intelligence, which is hilariously ironic because on my side it comes from a space of very little emotional intelligence. But it gives me direction, which enables me to act on what little I do have. Even if I don't have a lot in the first place.

Who knows how much of the world's knowledge is locked up in manuals that nobody's thought to read?

Our discussion then pivoted to another challenge for Jory, the give-and-take of conversation. We talked about the challenges of listening and responding, of back-and-forth exchanges, and of his struggles with interrupting—a struggle, I would note, that many people of all abilities have.

LW: After you started applying this manual's advice, did you notice a difference in how people responded to you?

JORY: People thought that I was a really good listener, and I was a good listener because part of the instructions tell you to make sure that you shepherd the conversation and not intrude, because intrusions can shut it down. The idea that people sometimes need time to think and don't need your response. Internalizing this did make me objectively a better listener, something that I'm still working on applying to situations that are not emotional.

One of the problems I have in normal conversations or intellectual conversations is that sometimes I interject. It's because if I don't say it more or less immediately, I'm going to lose it, my mind can't hold on to the idea if it's forced to be translated into language. I can't think of what to say and listen at the same time, but that leads to interrupting, which is bad in conversations.

LW: What's the hardest challenge between trying to formulate what you want to say and still staying current with the ongoing conversation?

JORY: So there are two challenges, the first of which is obviously if you miss something that was said, your response may not fully address something or, in the worst case, might be coming off as if you weren't paying attention fully to what they were saying. Because there definitely are people who only sort of half listen to what you're saying before pontificating about their great speech that they're going to give in reply. And I definitely don't want to be that person.

Then the second problem that can arise is that it can lead to a tendency to interrupt, in the sense that if I have a thought, if I don't speak it, it's gone. I have to weigh whether this contribution is valuable enough to interrupt, but I don't want to do that too often because then you are just interrupting people too often and that's no fun for them. On the other hand, I'll definitely forget it. Because then I'll be listening, and I'll totally lose what I meant to say, and I'll stay silent. It makes it tough, because it means I participate less or interrupt more, both of which are not really great.

LW: What is the challenge about holding or remembering thoughts? I would add that a lot of people struggle to varying degrees with that issue and with interrupting.

JORY: It makes sense that this wouldn't be just related to autism, but I think in my case it's probably exacerbated by the fact that when I translate thoughts into words, it takes a lot of mental processing. I have to work harder to think about how to appropriately phrase my ideas so they come off with some semblance of sense.

After I do, it's not saved where I can easily redo it. It's like after I do that each time, my brain needs the processing space back, so it deletes the bridge between the thoughts and words. Even if it's only twenty seconds later, the words have fallen off because they're no longer supported by anything mentally. Sometimes I'll be able to recover it, and surprise myself with, Oh, that's what I was going to say.

LW: You're always worried that people will misinterpret what you've said. But what are some of the ways that you might misinterpret things that are said to you? How does that work?

JORY: Mom will be the first to tell you that I do that. There are definitely bits where I will miss chunks of what people have said and not realize it. I think that's partly due to the fact that if I'm not solely focused on what somebody is speaking, that I'll miss it, which is tough in conversation because that means if I start trying to think of what I might like to say in reply, I'll miss the tail end of what they said.

Another related problem is that when anyone—myself included—presents an idea, there are always the assumptions that went into crafting their thinking. Other people might inherently understand these things better than me because they all think in a similar manner. But I don't automatically make the same assumptions. That's where the trouble comes in. Particularly with groups. Everyone else in the group can move forward, and I will be left behind. I may not even be aware that they've moved on. Later, I get confused. But I don't want to be stopping the group all the time and slowing things down.

LW: To put it another way, it's a dual-processing issue, trying to listen and follow their train of thought, while also formulating how you're going to respond.

JORY: Yes, it's very single track in the sense that I can't do both very well. Another way is that I will sometimes think people said one word and they actually said a similar word, but one that has a different meaning. In some cases, it can actually be pretty far off. That kind of misunderstanding or misinterpreting is a problem.

Then there's also the bit that if people say things that are especially loaded with emotional or other types of context dependencies, I will have a tendency to miss that.

I'm very bad at picking up sarcasm. In the past, people have said something sarcastic, and I've responded in a way that's not typical because I thought they meant what they said. I feel like those are really awkward moments for me.

LW: Which is easier for you to follow: a spoken argument or a speech, or a written document?

JORY: Before, I might have said that I preferred something written. But at this point, I would say that good writers and good speakers are kind of the same for me. I will respond to clarity and good communication, which can be evident in both or very much lacking in both. A really well-written book will probably beat a really good public speaker in most cases for me, but even a bad public speaker is much better than a very poorly written anything. I've been trying to make my way through a famous economics book, *The Wealth of Nations* by Adam Smith. It's just so dry. He's talking about grain prices, and there's nothing to make those ideas easier to grasp and assimilate. I can at least get something from people that are dry and not the best at speaking, but if it's a mind-numbingly boring book, I struggle with that.

5

Language Barriers

Talking about Language:

Decades of research have taught scientists that there is no single "language" spot inside the brain, but rather a complex circuitry that allows humans to express themselves through words. There are documented cases of people who have one form of aphasia—the medical term for language impairment—where they struggle to speak, versus another form where they string together long but highly random assortments of words. Brain researchers have postulated that most speech functions are primarily performed by two regions: Broca's area, discovered in 1861 by a French surgeon, Paul Broca, and Wernicke's area, named for German medical scholar Karl Wernicke, who identified it in 1874. To learn how to speak, infants and toddlers have to activate and connect these two main speech areas through a complex pathway of neurons. This process explains why babies can't speak and initially can't understand much of substance when someone speaks to them.

But that is hardly the end of the brain's language complexity. As with much of brain study, injury and affliction have provided the best maps of how volatile and complicated the connections are. There are stroke and brain injury victims who can recall nouns and not verbs, others who can hardly speak but have no trouble singing, and still others who can write sentences but cannot read them. For children on the autistic spectrum, language delay is a frequent struggle, and, conversely, language delays are often used as an early indicator of some type of autism. Two researchers, Catherine Wan and Gottfried Schlaug, have suggested trying to rethink autism by viewing it "as a disorder of connections between brain regions." They add that autistic language deficits may be due to "problems integrating" different brain functions, rather than with any impairment of these individual brain areas themselves.

This very brief tour of linguistic brain science provides a backdrop to Jory's descriptions of his own language struggles and how he eventually mastered the ability to communicate through speech. As his mother, Kelly, noted, when Jory began to speak, he often strung together words and phrases in ways that made no sense, or made no sense in context, such as asking to hear music by saying, "It's a cold night." Jory's brain had latched on to those words as being connected to music.

Jory begins by explaining why he sees language as a fundamental obstacle for him when it comes to communication.

JORY: A person who can walk might not even think about a tiny step, because they don't notice it, they don't have to take a large step up a stair. But for someone in a wheelchair, that bump is enough height to make an entrance inaccessible. I feel like people are usually surprised by that. Whereas, if somebody were to ask me that, I wouldn't say that a route is accessible unless I distinctly visualize the entire route. And in most cases I would re-walk it and check; I wouldn't just assume. Buildings are constructed by society, and the fact that people who are atypical have problems with something that they did not construct should surprise no one.

For me, it's not steps or buildings but language that gives me the most trouble. Part of the reason why I find language so difficult is because there is no alternative. If there was an alternative and perhaps other people were using it, I might be significantly better at communicating. And in particular, I'd be less likely to be misunderstood. I am always concerned about that. I try my best, but I also realize that many times I'm going to be tremendously irritated because there will be instances where I can't say something without it being misinterpreted, or I say something, and it will be misinterpreted and there's no way for me to correct it besides saying, "That's not what I meant at all." Which is challenging. Especially if everybody interprets it the same way, then they'll be suspicious and distrust me when I say that wasn't what I meant.

In some sense, language is continually being re-created, and most people think that's fine. There's not even any questioning of it by the larger society. But for me, those changes are like the small step no one notices. Then everyone else thinks I am wrong when I get stopped by the step.

LW: What would your ideal communication system be?
JORY: If I could create a default communication system for my

little circular world, it might be telepathy, something where you could instantly mind sync with anybody, and just pop in and out, and go everywhere and nowhere. But it's very hard to think about because it's not ever going to happen. If someone invented telepathy, it would probably be based on language. If I have trouble existing in everybody else's system, I guarantee everybody else would hate whatever system I might come up with. It would be terrible for everyone, except me and maybe other people with autism.

In my system, neurotypical people won't know how to communicate or translate what's going on in their mind and what's going on in the outside world. They wouldn't think it's stable; they'd think it's very chaotic. Nothing makes sense, and everything's very meaningless. It wouldn't solve the problem. It would be all the problems that I have, but in reverse for other people without autism.

The parts of language that are good shouldn't be changed just because I have difficulty with some of them. That's my personal opinion, I know that's not going to apply to everyone who feels a disconnect with language. And certainly, that same kind of logic doesn't hold for other social issues where people are disadvantaged or are excluded.

But in my case, I think it's fine. Yes, it leads to difficulties, but I don't think that's a problem because while I have a lot of difficulties and challenges, if I was offered the opportunity to swap to be like everyone else, I don't think I would. It's a trade-off that I am willing to accept.

LW: What is the biggest challenge for you when it comes to spoken language?

JORY: Most people learn a language by hearing it from the time they are babies. It is as if their brain does this weird thing and *bam!* all of a sudden, they start babbling, making sounds, and speaking. And then they can speak English or French or whatever language is spoken where they grew up. Babies who grow up in bilingual households can usually speak both languages. It's a natural, ingrained process. There is no other method of communication that they would have been better off using instead.

But for me, that's not the case. Everyone in my family, Mom especially, tried to communicate with me, but the progression had to occur on my end. I had speech therapy, which I don't remember, and I had Mom, who became a verifiable expert in Jory-speak. She could get through to me for what I needed to understand. My progression was the reverse; I had to gain control of my mind to be able to devote more effort and thought and energy to the communications bridge. In order to use words, I needed a parallel growth between my capacity to communicate and my willingness and ability to communicate.

In my case, ability was more important than willingness, because I was always willing to communicate with Mom even if I wasn't very good at it. It was a very slow, incremental progression. Mom was more or less constant in her ability to communicate with me—it was me having to learn that as I got better control of my mind and the energy available, then I could expend more effort in figuring out how do I translate this thing that I have in my brain into the medium that everybody else is using, which is language?

But I still struggle with the translation. From my perspective, when it comes to language, a huge chunk is missing. One of the worst parts is the ambiguity, how one word can mean several different things in different scenarios. Or how the same word can be pronounced differently—such as *live*, as in to be alive, and *live*, as in appearing now; or *wind* for the breeze and *wind* for a watch; or *tear*, as in cry, and *tear*, as in rip—and both words mean something different as a result. One word can mean up to three or four different things, depending on how it is used, like *bark* for a dog, or bark orders, or bark on a tree, or a bark, which is a type of ship. If you look at the *Oxford Dictionary* alone, there's going to be a couple of listings. And then if you think about the context, that could create another set of listings. And then if you think of the inflection and the syntax and the tone of voice, that's like three or four or five more shades of meaning or different meanings that you're adding for each individual word. It's horribly complicated. There should only be one word, one meaning.

Instead, I wonder why we even use words to describe something in the first place? Plato tried to use forms to communicate. You have no idea how much I agree with that sometimes. To me, words aren't complex; they are reductionist. Even hearing somebody say something actually does not help me the way it does for other people. Most people listen to somebody speaking, and they are basically sure they understand what that person thought. Well, for me, there's no hope of that.

Hearing a person say something can actually provide me with less information. Most people, when they hear a language they understand, probably can understand more than 50 percent of what the other person is thinking. (I do think many people assume they are better at listening and understanding than they actually are. They make a lot of mistakes.)

For me, it's not abysmal, it's not like 10 percent. But whatever you say, I have to translate into my own way of visual thinking and then translate it back again into language if I want to respond or add an idea. Each time I have to jump back and forth. I'm better now than I used to be simply because I've had more practice. I make that translation jump by comparing what I've heard in other instances. So I'll think, I'm pretty sure that person means this, because in these other scenarios, this was close enough. But I recognize that my baseline understanding is almost always going to be less than 50 percent. If I just try to wing it, if I don't put in some very hard work, I'm going to be wrong a majority of the time, where most other people are going to be right.

Communicating using email or text isn't better for me either. In that sense, I'm similar to other people. Seeing the other person speak gives you information. And the more useful things you have the better, I guess, even if it's only marginally useful data. Someone can send me a text message that expresses an emotional concern, and I won't pick up on it. I won't recognize it, and I definitely won't respond to it.

Given that Jory doesn't like language and his brain is not wired for words, how did he develop his language skills? The answer is years of speech therapy and practice. But, as we discussed, using language and being comfortable with using language are two very different things. Fundamental to Jory's communication with the outside world is his translation process, taking the concepts embedded in his "Jory beads" and trying to put them into words that can be understood by everyone else around him. His facility with language is also directly linked to his environment and his amount of mental energy.

JORY: Answering when I got comfortable with language is a tough question because one of the ways that autism affects me is that not only do I have to translate between what's in my brain and the language, but there's also this bit where if I'm in an environment where autism has more strength, such as a place with a lot of people, noise, and distractions, then I'm less capable of doing that translation. That area of my brain is reduced or slowed down in some way. If I'm in an environment that I really do not like, especially a new environment, I may not have all of my vocabulary available. I may speak slower. It may take me longer to process thoughts in a language way. I will have to think: What am I trying to say? And how do I say that, and then say it. I think more slowly as well. All of that is slower than normal and takes more energy. In a comfortable environment or one that I have been in before and is more familiar, I don't have much of a delay at all in terms of thinking about what I want to say, how to say it, and saying it. It's still me, but my language ability is substantially different between those two environments.

In terms of environment, I had to start out at the bottom of the curve. I could only deal with a few people, the people in my family, and then, over time, one friend, one neighbor, then my older brother Tyler's girlfriend. It was introducing one new person at a time. In the beginning, I really couldn't communicate with anyone beyond my family and my friend down the street, James, and Miss Nancy, who lived across from us.

Home school was also really the bottom of the curve. I

needed the space and time that Mom provided to develop. Once I was able to do that, Mom began to push me, adding small numbers of new people. She started in late middle school because she thought that I was ready. I certainly didn't agree at the time, but now, I look back and think that I was ready. It was similar to occupational and physical therapy and probably speech therapy, which I don't remember. A lot of those therapies were predicated on making me do things that I specifically did not want to do.

Mom strongly encouraged me to go to Youth Group and tennis lessons. I also started going to Club Day, which was like a homeschool cooperative, and I took British literature and math. But one thing that particularly stands out is Shakespeare Club. That was big for me because not only was I communicating, but I was communicating as a character, which gave me a lot of practice. I wasn't a great actor, but I could memorize the lines really well. In a costume, you can pretend you're somebody else. One of my favorite parts was being in the traveling band of misfits in *A Midsummer Night's Dream*, the people who stage the play and can't get anything right. I could do crazy stuff, and everyone was laughing.

Acting or public speaking in front of a group is much easier for me than being in most groups. Because onstage, you're not really having a social interaction. The audience is there, but you don't have to respond to the audience in the same way that you would in a large social group where everybody's milling around, and you have to pay attention to multiple people's body language, and it's hard to hear conversations—for me, especially. When you're a public speaker, you don't receive much facial feedback; it's vocal feedback, applause or boos or murmurs of agreement. I find that easier than most people probably would in comparison.

Translating ideas into words is always work for me, so when you remove some of the other tasks, it makes that one easier to do. Not that I don't find public speaking somewhat difficult, because I find all conversations slightly difficult.

LW: Is there such a thing for you as a comfortable conversation?
JORY: I wouldn't say my comfort level has been reduced, to be honest. But there's something about the more practice I've gotten, the less my brain has to work. With one specific person, I get to know them, and I have a database of their past comments or reactions, so I don't have to actively translate quite as much. For example, there's a big difference for me when I talk to Mom than when I encounter a stranger and we converse. I think familiarity with the person degrades annoying stimuli. When I'm talking to Mom, it takes less mental energy because instead of having to actively translate every single word that Mom says, I just assume she meant the same thing as last time she said that.

I think familiarity also applies to conversation generally. As a result of having more conversations, I found they used less energy. I wasn't overwhelmed with the negatives, and I could notice some of the positives. The balance shifts from being something that you want to avoid to something that in most cases you probably wouldn't want to avoid. Then I realized, Oh, this is potentially a new source of information, a new source of facts. Later in college, I learned if you listen more and shut up and let other people do some talking, they have data points you can ingest. So it is worth it being drained.

I realized too that even though my energy was drained from those interactions, with sleep it's going to recharge. That energy would be topped off the next morning, it's a renewable resource, so I can expend it.

LW: When did you become more comfortable with speaking and conversation?

JORY: My comfort level with other people really didn't start until college. I was heavily resistant to putting myself in situations with new people and new stimuli even as late as my freshman year of college. That first year, though, I did a lot more talking than I was used to because of the study program, Capstone Scholars, I was in at the University of South Carolina. I took a freshman seminar, and then second semester, I took a leadership course, and both involved a lot of talking. But it was with a very nice group, and the professor was the same professor for both, which helped, and he was a good facilitator, a mentor.

The other piece is right before I started freshman year, I got Daisy, my service dog. Everybody on campus had left their dogs at home and was emotionally wrecked. Somehow, all their dogs looked like Daisy. I swear I had people say, "Daisy reminds me of my little dog." I'd ask, "What kind of dog?" "A Chihuahua." I'd be like, What? It's not even similar—there's like a fifty-pound size difference. It was interesting at times, but way more people talk to you and eventually I discovered that was nice. Because I was not very good at initiating conversation. By freshman year, I would converse, but I would rarely initiate conversations unless I already knew the person. That changed with Daisy because tons of people were initiating conversations with me.

After a year of that, I got a lot of practice—unwanted practice—but I began to appreciate it because then I thought,

Well, maybe I should do things like join the Marine Science Club, which my faculty advisor, Jean, had helpfully suggested. Sophomore year, that's what I did. It was great, I really enjoyed it. By junior year, I started doing things without having them be suggested. I did them on my own at a ridiculous pace. It was that kind of progression. The journey started pretty late, but it occurred.

From starting at the bottom of the curve, today I'm able to interact with completely different people. I can handle more types of people, more strangers, more environments. It's not totally destabilizing.

Since language is a struggle, Jory and I discussed what communication strategies are helpful to him so that he can better process language. But while the suggestions are "Jory-specific," they are universal enough that they could apply to other people with language-processing issues, even those not on the autism spectrum.

JORY:

1. Use observation and variety. I respond well to both observation and variety. If you're talking about an idea, and I can see the idea in action, that's good. Let me observe it directly. For example, if you are trying to tell me how to use a new type of vegetable slicer or some other kitchen tool. If you can't let me see it directly, then help me triangulate

it by talking about it in multiple ways. Explain to me how you visualize something and then also tell me about it. That way, I will have two different ways of trying to translate. Using more than one method helps me reduce errors or misinterpretation.

2. Use repetition. I'm definitely helped by repeating ideas, concepts, statements, and directions. Regardless of what the idea or concept is, I still have to translate it into Jory beads to use it internally. If I can cross-check it a little bit or hear it a few times, then there's slightly less of a chance of miscommunication.

3. Avoid dual meanings. I have a lot of difficulty with phrases that either have a dual meaning or where the majority of the meaning comes from emotions. Phrases such as "he can't help himself," "I'm not buying it," or "it doesn't hurt to." Otherwise I'm going to miss the full meaning because I don't have the context which most people have, whether that's emotional or something else. Or at least if you inform me of that meaning, then it goes a really long way to helping me interpret it. For me, not only are the connotations of words difficult but also the denotations are difficult. I think a lot of denotations actually require subconscious processing. And I don't understand and probably won't get sarcasm at all.

4. Avoid assumptions. Leaving things unsaid is very hard for me. That tends to happen when it's about a common cultural thing. Idioms and figures of speech often test me

because I won't automatically recognize it as a figure of speech, and I'll have to process that. "Bent out of shape," "speak of the devil," "two peas in a pod," phrases along those lines have been difficult for me to understand. If a person uses a lot of phrases like that, I might miss the overall picture. If there's only one or two, it's okay.

5. Use words, not body language. If you rely on body language or gestures, and especially if those are conveying the opposite meaning from what you are saying, I won't pick up on it. Don't communicate with lots of nonword signals that I am supposed to "pick up on."

6. Avoid speaking too fast. Rapid-fire speech is something that I have trouble with. Either speak at a reasonable pace or pause for a few seconds every now and again to let me catch up in case I'm still processing.

Knowing that every conversation is energy draining, how does Jory make the most of the conversations that he has? What for him is a worthwhile conversation? What might it be for any of us?

LW: What do you like to talk about?

JORY: One thing I don't like is small talk. I don't like to talk about the weather; I like to talk about nerdy, intellectual stuff. I'm a big news follower, so any news of the day will interest me. But I've found conversations about people's backgrounds or why they think the way they do based on their prior experiences to be very interesting. What differentiates those things from small talk is that there is some value being shared. It doesn't have to be vulnerable or personally revealing. But I feel like it's a different kind of conversation because you walk away from that learning something.

LW: And who is worth having a conversation with?
JORY: I don't want to hang out with people who are not nice. Because there is definitely a sense that who you surround yourself with helps you grow in some sense. I wouldn't want to be in an environment all the time where people are super cynical or hate everyone. I generally find a wide range of people pretty interesting as long as they meet the basic criteria of not being a terrible person and talking at least some of the time about something other than the weather or what they ate for breakfast.

I do enjoy hanging out with people that I know, but usually less so at bars or any party-type atmosphere, because those environments are not as easy for me to be in. It also comes down to the fact that a party with alcohol will reduce everybody's intelligence level slightly. Although at Oxford, weirdly enough, there are all sorts of intellectual parties.

Generally speaking, I've found that I'm very bad at initiating activities, so I'm very bad at bringing people together. But if people are getting together, if I'm not already doing something, usually I'll go unless I'm especially tired. When my course mates organize something at a coffee shop, if I'm not busy, I'll stop by for thirty minutes. One to two hours is my typical limit unless we're doing something specific like playing board games or there's extra structured engagement or a discussion. I go weekly to the chapel lunch club for theological matters for close to two hours. That kind of discussion is fine, and I could probably stay a little bit longer. But if it's an event at the graduate student lounge where they're having a bar night, I might spend thirty minutes.

Paradoxically, Jory and I spent quite a few minutes discussing what he finds so onerous about small talk. But as he spoke, and I listened, there was also a part of my mind that began to wonder how often many of us miss out on more meaningful conversations because we immerse ourselves in narrow, more superficial topics. Or how often do people try to escape from a tedious companion by in essence saying, "So tell me more about yourself," or "Tell me more about what you think about this"?

JORY: When people ask about a standard set of things like work or the weather or what you did on the weekend, it's less that they are interested in what is being said than in simply keeping the conversation going. I find that pretty difficult, to be honest, and pretty draining. Continually keeping up with draining conversation, where there's nothing to keep me engaged, is not impossible but it's hard. And the longer it goes on, the harder it is. I'm good at small talk as long as it doesn't last more than ten minutes. But that's bad if you're having a dinner with someone and the small talk lasts for two hours. That's where I run into a lot of problems.

Sometimes I may come off as just not very good at conversations because after a while I'll have to stop and recharge a little bit. If it's not going to move out of small talk, I'll at least ask some question so the other person or the group can hopefully talk about it for a long period of time.

6

Language Disconnect

Talking about All the Ways That Language and Communication Can Be Misunderstood:

Along with learning the mechanics of speech, all of us have to learn "how" to speak. This "how" revolves around social cues, what is acceptable to say and what isn't, and how communication conveys not only words but the mental and emotional state of the person speaking. Neurotypical people absorb this information from the time they are babies; their neurons take repeated experiences and translate them into increasingly accurate predictions of someone else's emotions and state of mind, via a largely unconscious process. This is how most of us can detect subtle changes in meaning and sort through nonverbal clues about emotions. By contrast, Jory is very aware of the step-by-step nature of this process for himself.

JORY: I'm not as good at learning by experience, so it takes me more experiences to understand the same thing. At some point, I will have had enough experiences where I'm able to preset a filter or an additional mental loop to be aware. I want to be respectful of the way everybody else tends to think—not that everybody else thinks the same way, but there are some similarities.

If the exact same thing has happened, I wouldn't need more than one or two times to learn. But if it involves an emotion, like somebody was offended or hurt by something said, that's a very nuanced thing. Two situations where a similar reaction might arise can have very little in common except for the fact that there's a conversation occurring. For me to understand that circumstance, I would need quite a few actual examples. For some of the super-nuanced ones, I'm not any better even after many examples.

For example, language that is racist has much more similarity in terms of the words used, so I wouldn't need many instances to recognize when somebody said something racist toward someone else. But a more subtle event, such as when one person is being dismissive of another in a conversation, that's still something I don't pick up on very well. I've tried to train myself to be more observant, so I might miss the language bit but notice the body posture reaction bit. But I'll have no idea what exactly happened, which is pretty typical. I won't remember what the specific words were, I'll only know that they were impactful for someone else.

What makes a conversation complicated is anything related to body posture. If somebody's indicating by nonverbal means that they feel a certain way, but they don't ever give you any indication or they use language that says the opposite, that's very hard. I could ask someone, "Are you okay?" They may say yes, but their posture is saying the opposite. It's terrible. Unless I'm observing that there's a disconnect between their language and the posture they're portraying with their limbs, I might just assume that they're telling the truth, and make a horrible assumption. I might be super cheery, and just totally steamroll over them, and make their day much worse because I didn't catch those cues. Where everyone else would know to say, "Are you sure? I'm here for you if you want to talk."

I've noticed that if I'm interacting with somebody one-on-one where fewer signals are being sent, I have a better chance of picking up on them, as compared to a group conversation, where somebody's joke may have made someone laugh at the joke but may have also made somebody else feel bad. Signals coming from three or more different people at the same time make it a lot harder. Even if I'm only the fourth person, and I'm doing nothing, it makes it harder because my eyes can't be everywhere at once.

In addition to nonverbal cues, Jory also struggles with the larger cultural contexts of language. He has a lot of questions, many of which also highlight some of the fundamental assumptions most neurotypical people make when we communicate. He wants to know: Why don't people in the US and people in the United Kingdom speak the same, if they are both speaking English? Why does anyone give more weight or value to what a celebrity says? Why do people adopt someone else's words as their own? These are assumptions worth questioning, whether or not you have autism.

JORY: I can learn the rules of the game, but the rules don't make sense to me. If you can make an assumption based on culture or the understood social contract, and then do things subconsciously, you speed up things. But from my perspective, I can't look up "social contract" on the Internet and have some document tell me what it is. It's all assumed; it's all subconscious, and it's reenvisioned and reedited all the time. There seem to be multiple versions of these contracts for different things, which combine to make it into a culture. But for me it's just very strange. When I came from the US to the UK, it was confusing to me that there's a difference.

In my mind, everybody is different from everybody else, and so why would specific locations do things one way, and then in another location, it's entirely different? Even across a very short distance, there can be a different social contract.

I find that very hard to understand because in my mind not only do you have the confusion of why would you even do that in the first place, but then there's an additional layer of confusion because there's no uniformity. It's as if when you use a computer, you never know which way to plug in the cord because the plug location has been switched or it looks different or it had a different shape, and so it takes you forever to figure out where to plug in your power cable. That's why industry standards are adopted. It makes it easy and makes it simple. But in terms of communication, for me, it seems as if everybody knows there's a standard and I'm the only one who's saying, "What standard are y'all talking about?" There's no standard here. I wasn't invited to the deliberating conference that set out the standard. I'm just not part of this club. But I try to get by. I can still observe culture and still take notes on it and hope it doesn't change too much.

This discussion of language differences then led us to speak about how our larger society treats words and ideas. Jory shared his views on the concept of what is an independent idea and asked why people are often so quick to give more weight to a celebrity's words than those of a nonfamous person.

JORY: What really stands out for me is that I don't understand the whole process of people hearing language and then they adopt it for themselves. Later, you ask them for their thoughts about something, and they'll just repeat someone else's thoughts that they already heard. Except now they think that these are their own thoughts.

Why on earth would you think that just because someone else—especially a person you don't know—said something, it's true? I can almost tell whether a person has independently thought about an idea themselves in any capacity. If it's coming from somewhere else, it sounds different.

People also respond to another person's ideas depending on how they are presented. I'm not able to do that. I recognize that if you're emotionally connected to this issue, you may respond to someone else who has very strong opinions, but in the same way I would never assume that someone speaking without passion has no passion about the topic. I would treat both people identically, even though they speak differently, because both of them are strangers to me.

Responding to language and to what is said are definitely areas where I diverge from a good number of people—they respond to strangers as if they knew them because of rhetoric, which seems to me kind of bonkers. I am confused as to why people

follow celebrity figures and why their words become more pow-
erful simply because of who they are and the fact that they are
famous. Why do people assume that being famous equates to
having good character, more intelligence, or automatically being
deserving of more respect? Because when you give more weight
to what someone who is famous says, this also means that another person's words automatically carry less weight and have
less power, even if they are the exact same words.

So I find people's reactions a little bit odd because I'm like,
Why would you think that about this person that you don't know?

LW: Why is it good to be of two minds about an idea?
JORY: I don't form opinions about language I receive. Each verbal concept has to become compressed into a Jory bead, to be
translated first, before I can understand it. It's not a merger of
yourself with either someone else or with an idea that is outside
of yourself. When I take ideas and things into my mind, each
one is kind of quarantined so that this one idea cannot infect or
override other ideas.

That separation is often viewed as bad. If you're of two minds
about something, people sometimes think of that as duplicitous,
or if you hold two even remotely opposing ideas quarantined in
your mind like that, people will assume that you're in the middle,
or you're not invested in either one or the other, because you hav-
en't picked one to the exclusion of the other. And I respond, maybe
for you, but not for me. It's an area that has been the most difficult
for me to communicate to others. They are in identical beads, but
they are not the same, and I don't necessarily treat them the same.
Some may be true or more important. Sometimes I wonder how

people can make sense of ideas if they are different in the mind, because then your mind would have to take a defined shape.

I asked Jory to give me a list of ten words that make sense and don't make sense to him. Here is his list, with his commentary attached:

WORDS THAT DON'T MAKE SENSE:

1. *So*—I was listening to a podcast and they were talking about how the word so is particularly important in human communication; it lets more complex ideas be expressed or something like that. But it just seems like such a nonsense word in the sense that it's not relevant. If it was removed, I would have no trouble following a logical argument.
2. Words that are onomatopoeia, words that are supposed to be like sounds, I don't understand those. Why wouldn't you just do the sound?
3. Idioms, such as "cold feet" or "raining cats and dogs."
4. Swear words because I would rather have somebody competently express their displeasure using a greater vocabulary. (And I think asking me for ten examples is a high number.)

WORDS THAT MAKE SENSE:

1. *Ramble*. I tend to like words that are descriptive in the sense that they're really simplistic in relating to specific things.

Ramble really just means walking, but it fosters an image for you. I like words like that because it's a little bit easier to make the translation process to images, if the word is giving an image already. Descriptive words connect right to an image.

2. *Pillow*. I like the word *pillow* because a lot of the letters are kind of poofy, like o's and *w* and *p*. They all slightly resemble a pillow, which I find somewhat amusing.

3. *Trill*. Even though I don't like onomatopoeia, I do like some words that describe sounds, like *trill*, which is often used to describe bird calls. It's a strange word, but it does tell you something.

4. Every so often, I'll see a word that's unusual where its meaning is hyperspecific. There's a website I like and one time the author built a kind of typewriter program that would limit you to write with the top 1,000 most-used English words—the list had words like *as*, *is*, *such*, *he*, *hot*, *for*, *that*, *one*, *be*. It was surprisingly difficult to write anything, but at the same time you could write out some really complex stuff if you thought about it. It made me realize that a large number of words on that top 1,000 list are words I do not like and do not understand. And I think because they're used so frequently, the context in which they are used also shifts frequently and it's hard to pin any of them down. Versus rare words, which are like a spice in the kitchen which is only used in a couple of your recipes, but it makes those recipes really fantastic. Most of

the words are like that thing you eat every day and you're tired of.

5. *Brook.* It's hyperspecific, because a brook is not a stream and it's not a river and so forth.

Forms of Storytelling: Maps and Charts versus Words

Personally, I think charts and maps can be much better at telling a story than people are in some ways. People make the maps, but it takes less words. You make a nice map and you show it to somebody and they're like, Oh, yeah, that makes sense. That's good. Then you know you've improved somebody's understanding—and it's their own understanding because they used their own parts of their brain to unlock that. You didn't have to force it into them.

LW: Have you ever tried to learn another language, like French or Spanish?

JORY: I took Spanish in high school, and then the University of South Carolina had a language requirement, so I took two semesters of college-level Spanish as well, but I can't speak Spanish. I think it would be nice to learn another language. In terms of how challenging it is, it's about the same for me with any language. I had one conversation with a student sitting next to me in a Spanish class. They were saying how hard it is because the voice in your head is in English, so it's hard to speak Spanish. That was not a problem for me because I had neither Spanish nor English going on in my head.

But for me speaking was just as challenging as it was for them. The one thing I gained from Spanish is that I can sort of read it, if it's not too complicated, especially signs. I can sort of deduce what the Spanish might mean.

Even with English, I thought it would be worse when I came to the UK, I thought this is going to be terrible because they speak British. But it actually turned out to be pretty good, because I struggle with both US and UK English.

Jory often experiences the assumption that two autistic people must be on the same wavelength and have an easier time communicating. In fact, he has found it to be the opposite, and he explains why, to him, two autistic people aren't necessarily great communicators with each other:

LW: Do you ever feel as if you have a better connection or a better rapport more quickly with someone else who is autistic?

JORY: If anything, it's probably harder. Because language is the means of communication, not telepathy. If you're trying to connect with another person using the bridge of language, then when you talk with a non-autistic person, you can easily expect one-half of the bridge to operate the way the default is set. But heaven forbid if both sides of the bridge are expecting the other side to be operating on the default state, and instead, it's somebody else on the spectrum. Then both sides of the bridge have problems, rather than simply one side. I've definitely found it more challenging to communicate with another person on the spectrum in most cases because we are both struggling. However, in many cases it usually works out fine, because nobody is making assumptions and using specific language. There's also usually much less small talk.

Books are a different experience than conversation for Jory. As he puts it, "When I read a book, it doesn't drain me in the same way as a conversation."

JORY: I remember one book, *A Child's History of the World*, that used very simple language, which was very helpful, obviously. It was a story that was being told, and language was the only medium that the author had available. I think it is a subtle but very important distinction. Up until that point, I could understand things that Mom was talking about, but I didn't see the connection between knowledge and books. But this book was very clearly and intentionally written, so you were just experiencing the story because of how simply it was written. There was a lot there, but it was not hard to gain access to. Which was particularly important for me, because I hadn't reached a point where maybe I could interpret a more traditional history textbook or something like that very well.

Reading it, I got the idea that facts, when put together with other facts, can be really, really interesting. After that, I must have subconsciously decided to acquire loads of facts, like data points. And that has stuck with me, that desire to know more things. The more I learn about things, the more I discover what I don't know, which is infuriating. But the process of increasing your knowledge is something I like. After I read that book, it was sort of turning on a switch that has stayed on. I had more motivation to do the harder stuff and seek out more language.

LW: Book versus conversation, which do you prefer?

JORY: That's too simplistic. If it's a good book versus like a conversation about the weather, I'll 100 percent like the book. But if we're talking about something interesting, then I might prefer that to a book because a book can be one-sided and not dynamic. Writers can sometimes be so obsessed with the genius of their own ideas that it kind of comes off the wrong way.

If it's the kind of conversation where something interesting and unexpected happens, it's awesome. But if that's not the type of conversation, then I'd prefer a book.

There are plenty of books where you don't feel the presence of the writer. You feel the story, especially those books that transport you to another place, whether that's an idea or whether it's more for fun, like sci-fi or a mystery. That element doesn't occur very often in conversations.

I can never quote movies or books like some people can. But if I've read something and paid attention to it and enjoyed it, then I can give you a full description. Although oftentimes, I'll ignore large chunks of the author's descriptions of the characters and the places and things like that. Movies are always a surprise to me if I've read the book. I do a lot more imagining in my own head about what something looks like and rely less on the author's words that they've worked so hard to stick in there about somebody's appearance.

Along with his different reading style, Jory has a different style of learning. Here, he talks about why he doesn't reread and why he doesn't take notes during lectures.

JORY: One thing I hardly ever do is reread something I've read. If I was paying attention while I read a book, I'm not going to learn anything new if I come back later, even in a different part of my life. Once it's in my brain, that channel of information is done, you can't dredge it any deeper. I've tried it a few times, but it's obvious that's not how my brain works, so I don't bother doing something that it's not set up for. But I do have recall. Whenever something relevant is said in a future conversation, I'll remember what I read.

With more interesting material, I do have interruptions, if you will, from my brain. I'll read something and my brain immediately starts making connections to things I've thought about for a while or random problems. You might call it distractibility, but I wouldn't call it a loss of concentration because if anything I concentrate harder, just not on the text anymore. My brain just got kicked into overdrive on another topic because it is interesting.

LW: When you're listening to a lecture, do you take notes? Or do you divide your brain up into spoken versus written communication?

JORY: I discovered that my best notes were no notes. If I simply listened to the professor, I did much better. Taking a break from listening to write things down interrupted the stream and it would take me a long time to get back into listening mode again—the translation for the listening was different from the translation for writing down. If I'm paying attention in class, I'm taking good notes, just in my mind.

Talking about Likes and Dislikes:

Jory does not lack for strong opinions when it comes to his likes and dislikes, the latter of which span shopping malls, fashion, and cable news debates. He was rarely excited when I tried to wheedle lists out of him, but we both enjoyed making this set—in fact, in the lists, we got to twelve and thirteen, respectively—and it was accompanied by a fair amount of laughter. See how much you agree or disagree.

LW: What are ten things that you like?
JORY: Ten things that I like, as in personally?

1. News media, specifically newspapers
2. Podcasts
3. Coca-Cola
4. Birds
5. Nature, generally. How many do I have?

LW: We are up to five. Five more to go.
JORY: All right. Shoot. Mentioned nature.

6.   Coffee
7.   Chatting with people over coffee, if I know them. Not like strangers, but friends.
8.   Nerdy stuff. Can I put a specific place? (Yes.)
9.   Congaree National Park in South Carolina
10. Worcester College in Oxford. Those are two places that I really enjoy. One from home and one from England.
11. I like ocean earth science. It's really practical. Something like studying the multiverse doesn't seem very practical to me. Not that other people shouldn't do impractical science because there are many ways that investment in science has great benefits for society. But it's just not for me personally. Other people can study the multiverse and have a good time. And then they can tell me about it.
12. I've always liked Martin Luther King's speeches because he uses language that does have a lot of interesting things in it, but is very easy to follow and interpret. He talks about ideas that are really big ideas in many cases, but he grounds them in the context of whomever he's speaking to, or creates imagery for people to latch on to, or gets them to think about their life experiences and connects that to American ideals.

LW: Ten things that you don't like or avoid.
JORY:

1. The mall.
2. Concerts; specifically loud music concerts. I do like some kinds of music and going to plays and stuff.
3. Those terrible beverages that are sugar-free. Those are just terrible. Actually, the other day at the store I almost made the mistake of buying a zero-sugar Coke.
4. Emotional rhetoric, I'll put in that one.
5. Public intellectuals/pundits. Anybody whose job it is not to do anything but tell other people what they think.
6. Conversations that don't mean anything, small talk, I guess.
7. The general mindset of egoisms, especially elitism. Those bother me.
8. People that are not nice to either animals or people whom they think are beneath them in whatever way. What do we have now, two left? (Yes.)
9. People that don't smell flowers.
10. Fashion. I do not understand fashion. Like I'll think something looks nice, and Mom will say, "No, you've got to change." I'm like, "Why?" And she says, "Those colors are too close together." Because you apparently can't have pants and a shirt that are too close in color or whatever. Or pattern on top of pattern. All these rules. They're terrible. They don't make any sense at all.

Jory also does not much care for

11.   Humor.
12.   Music.
13.   Cable news debates.

He explains why.

JORY: If you put a funny stand-up comedian on, I'll probably laugh but I don't know. Humor to me is more fun when it's with friends, even if it's really bad humor, like texting puns back and forth. I think that's kind of funny. But with a comedian, I don't know this person, I don't have any connection to this person. If I laugh, it doesn't have any meaning behind it. It has more memory value if it comes from people I know. Sometimes, Mom will send me some funny clip from John Oliver or *Saturday Night Live*, but if I'm thinking, What can I watch on Netflix?, it's never put on some comedy, it'll be put on a documentary.

LW: What forms of humor are really not funny to you?
JORY: Some humor doesn't make sense. The whole bit about laughing at other people's apparent or real injuries is always confusing. Like the *Looney Tunes*–style where the coyote just got blown up with dynamite again. I'm like, What? It's so weird to me that it's culturally ingrained, that blowing up random animals with TNT is humorous. Or on TV, if somebody trips and face-

plants, there's a laugh track in the background. That's not funny. If they have a nosebleed or hit their head or something. Why is it societally ingrained to laugh at personal injury? It's not funny. Nothing about it should be that humorous.

LW: Is there any other type of entertainment that you don't enjoy?

JORY: I'm not a fan of a lot of music. Even music that I do like, I won't listen to independently on my phone. I really love the music of chapel Evensong, but if you loaded a bunch of Evensong songs on my iPhone, I would not listen to them. To me, reading a book or watching something on TV or a movie or staring at birds outside, even just thinking silently and reflecting, is more entertaining than listening to digital music. And I can't really explain why that is. I can appreciate good singing in person.

I will listen to digital podcasts. I really enjoy them because I can learn something new. I mostly listen to political and economic podcasts. I can acquire additional information that I wouldn't get otherwise, which is kind of neat.

But Jory draws the line at cable news or news talk show debates, which he does not like.

JORY: I've never really understood why people watch news segments where they have four or five people in boxes, and they just yell at each other, and that's all that happens. They have a list of talking points, but no complex thoughts or discussion. That's always been very confusing to me.

I've never been able to understand arguments very well. People will say after a debate, that was a really good argument. To me, all speech sounds functionally the same, regardless of how impressive it is. There are all of these channels of information that I am apparently unable to pick up on or learn from.

LW: What about social media? What do you think about it?

JORY: I don't like it because I see how it encourages ideologies and rhetoric, and I dislike both. Ideologies and rhetoric are two of the worst aspects of communication for me. Too many people on social media are very good at making you think whatever they want because of their word choice and by inciting an emotional response. If it's in person, you can ask actual questions where they can't evade.

But people who do rhetoric for a living can trap you in an endless cycle of communication which has no meaning. Both sides of any debate these days have become very good at it, seemingly. And they're employing it across social media on a mass scale. It's like you're seeing a painting that somebody specifically painted just for you. With varying nefarious intentions.

Sometimes I think social media is really great, it opens a channel for many people to communicate. But sometimes it's really bad, and it's clear that people are also very bad at communicating with each other. Sometimes, I read the online exchanges and I wonder who truly struggles with communication here.

7

Personality Is a Choice

Talking about Personality:

A key component in how Jory interacts with the world is through personality. But he views personality in a very different way from most neurotypical people. Most people tend to view personality as something innate, which we are largely born with. Jory, however, views personality as a choice.

He describes it as a feature that he has worked to construct internally, in order to relate better to the neurotypical people around him. His personality of choice may surprise you. He has chosen Ruthless Optimism.

JORY: For most people, their environment and culture shape the components of their identity in some ways. Things are acting to shape you, as you shape the world. Whereas for me, that's not really the case. It's more of a disconnect. My response to the world is modulated by my intellectual thoughts, which is not really a great way to interact with the world because the world's not set up for that. But if the world is not set up for me to interact with it, that also means I can just do whatever I want, right?

My choice about how to be is a reflection of what I find optimal from the intellectual perspective. I've chosen ruthless optimism as how I present myself.

Many people might think it's an odd choice. I feel like, rightly in many cases, a lot of people with disabilities are closer physically to what some might refer to as a state of suffering. For me, I picked the opposite, which is being weirdly cheerful, but it is my intellectual choice. None of us lives forever at least in terms of this life, and I have a limited subset of years. The things I see myself working toward are really well served by ruthless optimism.

People will say that I'm very cheerful or I'm very "unstressed," but because I think personality has a lot to do with emotional characteristics and because I don't have any emotional characteristics, in my opinion—or very few and they are very dampened—I shift my personality. I have states that I switch between. I feel like if I explain it, it always comes off as kind of creepy because it sounds fake. But whereas other people just have a personality, I have to construct one. My default is very dry and unperturbed and intellectual. But if I'm in a group and especially if I'm with friends, I have a more bubbly, cheerful persona. I probably smile too much as a part of that. The way my brain works is to tell my face to keep smiling. I also have kind of a more outgoing side, lame humor, lame puns. And I have a public speaking persona where I'm speaking and I know people are listening. It's like I put on different masks, you know? Because it's not really me. It's just the mask.

Everybody else uses language and personality to communicate—I have to do that to communicate as well. But because I didn't really have a set pattern, I sort of just created some. And it works pretty well.

Without that creation, my personality would be the same in all situations, which is weird, because people aren't that way. People react to their environment. They react to other people. They react to all sorts of things. I don't want to come off as weirdly robotic, so I decided it's better to have a personality that's more serious and friendly and intellectual and another that's bubbly and dorky and witty.

When I don't use these personalities, it leads to more problems with language. For instance, sometimes when I'm with Mom, I will be more robotic and end up hurting her feelings because my tone is just very cold and flat. She'll tell me, it wasn't what you said, it was the tone. I'll realize I wasn't masking enough.

It can happen too if I'm using more of my brain in an intellectual discussion. I'll be slightly more robotic; my voice will have no modularity and my facial expressions will be nonexistent. The reason why that happens is because it takes a bit of mental effort to make the facial muscles move and be expressive. But typically, I'll move in and out of that. Because it's important, and when it's missing, things don't go well.

I don't talk about choosing personalities with other people because it's weird; it has many ways of coming across as disingenuous. Definitionally, I suppose, it is deception, since it's not how I would otherwise be. But I think it's a pretty harmless choice in the sense that it helps me interact with people a little better.

Monotone speech has long been considered a hallmark of autism. Jory explains why he is likely to speak in a monotone.

JORY: I typically don't add things like inflections to my speech, so I'll sound horribly monotone like when I'm talking to Mom sometimes. In one instance, we were talking, and it didn't come off very well because she assumed I was bulldozing her ideas with my monotone voice, indicating that I didn't consider her ideas to have merit, on a small thing, like the price of something. I was speaking like a feelingless robot, and it hurt her feelings. But once I explained that it was the end of the day, and I didn't have much energy left over, Mom realized why I was speaking that way. I felt bad about not putting in extra effort.

That goes back to how we start a conversation. People like to attribute all sorts of actions to autistic behavior. But a lot of times people are bad at attributing the very few things that are primarily a result of autism. Like that conversation with Mom, which is tough, because I can envision how it is difficult for somebody to fully understand and predict my behavior, to understand what I'm thinking or not thinking.

Talking about the Senses: Sight and Smell:

Sensory issues, specifically sensory integration, are often a challenge for people on the autistic spectrum. The stimuli that a neurotypical person might find annoying, an autistic person can find overwhelming. We talked about what Jory likes and does not like to look at and to smell to offer a window into what stimuli are too much. And then he asked me a question about how I see.

LW: What are things you like and don't like to look at?
JORY: I hate to say it, but really artsy stuff I don't get. Like mod-

ern art or that art where it's abstract and you're supposed to bring meanings from something. My nephew could probably do that if we gave him some paint. I've looked at art exhibits in London and Paris, and sometimes I think this work is terrible. I do struggle with art. I do appreciate it sometimes—but I don't really understand it. There are some cases where I'll be captivated by a particular artwork, but many times I get the feeling they were made by and for people who don't think like me.

I enjoy looking at nature. Especially birds and ocean things.

I do like looking at people's ears and eyes. I don't know why ears, but eyes—people are very good at communicating with their eyes. They're not deceptive with their eyes, usually. So that's nice. And the same with ears because people can't change their ears very much. Although I—it feels really bad to say—but I don't like when people have those funny earrings that make big holes in their ears. I can't ignore it, but it always gets me every time. For a few seconds, I'm like, Oh! And then I'm like, Oh, yes, that is a thing people do. And then I laugh at myself, and then it's fine.

I don't enjoy looking at aspects of people that are complicating, like fashion or hairstyles or any other personal styling.

I like the newspaper, the widths of the columns and the typesetting and so forth. I appreciate that. Those things that somebody paid very specific attention to, but almost nobody else notices. I definitely appreciate the nice way a newspaper looks and how it all fits and so forth.

I like looking at sort of odd mechanical things, chains or those funky MacGyver machines people make and put on the Internet and so forth. I find those quite fun to look at. There's the whole subgenre of videos by people who make really long courses for marbles. They're quite entertaining.

I like looking at pictures from another continent or stuff in the anthropology museum like Polynesian canoes. It's really interesting, the shapes and the symbols, the way that it's designed, it feels different looking at it.

I don't like looking at crowds or portraits of people.

LW: Let's talk about smells that you like and don't like.

JORY: Smells that I like. Birds. Particularly their downy feathers. It's a very nice smell.

I have smelled a baby, and generally find babies quite strange and then weird and slightly off-putting. But baby smell is surprisingly pleasant, which is very strange. I feel like I'm being tricked by biology but whatever. That's fine.

I like flower smells but not replications of flower smells like in soap or shampoo. They never quite get it right, so I put it on the "do not like" list. But on the "like" list is actual flowers. It's quite nice to get some flowers and stick them in the kitchen.

Sap from Christmas trees. Have you ever smelled that?

LW: Yes.

JORY: It's a good smell. I think cinnamon smells quite nice for some reason, like among the spices. I also kind of like the smell of garlic in a weird way. How many was that?

LW: Six. Can you think of two more?

JORY: I think sometimes teas smell nice; particularly rooibos tea smells really good. Other teas smell okay, but that one smells really good for some reason. And a plain candle, just a plain bees-wax candle. Scented candles can get it right, but sometimes they also get it wrong. It's all those chemical scents. But beeswax candles do smell good. They're not scented, but they do have a smell.

LW: Okay, what are some smells that you really dislike?

JORY: Well, sadly for Daisy, wet dog does not have a great smell. Goose poop also. There are a lot of geese around Oxford. If it's just on the ground it doesn't smell, but as soon as you step in it, it smells terrible. I mentioned fake flower smell. Another smell that I do like is peppermints and spearmint, as well, but they're similar. Generally speaking, I feel like attempts to replicate nat-ural smells like trees or flowers in fake form don't tend to work out, at least for me.

I don't like the smell of spilled alcoholic beverages such as beer, which is weird because generally when they're in a glass it's fine. But for some reason when they're spilled it smells real bad.

Then that sort of sewage smell that sometimes lofts out of drainage grates if it's been raining a lot or something.

And lots of intermixing human body odors—the smell of people past a certain critical threshold. They might even be rel-atively hygienic people. But if there's enough of them—at some point it just smells like people. I find it funny that individually they may smell good, but together they smell different.

And then fruit that has gone bad, but you don't know it until you open it.

JORY: So I'm going to ask you a question. When you blink, do you see black? A normal-speed blink, that happens when you're going about your day. You're just walking around. Do you see tiny blips of black all the time?

LW: No. Because I'm not conscious of it. But if you make me think about it and you ask me to think about it, which you just did, I will become conscious of it, and I will see it.

JORY: If you think about it, okay. Apparently about an hour of every waking day goes by in literal blinks, and your brain just stitches things together and you never recognize the absence of what you don't see while you blink. But I see the black space when I blink, and if I miss anything because I blinked, I'm like what are you talking about? It's annoying. I go through that all the time. I can't just turn it off.

8

Things That Matter

Talking about Friendship:

As a child, friendship was elusive for Jory. He had one good friend, James, who lived down the block. In high school and college, Jory began to expand that group. But he still finds genuine friendship a challenge—however, the heartfelt genuineness of his vision of friendship could in many ways be seen as a challenge for all of us.

What is true friendship? What do we ask of our friends and what do we hope for from our friendships? What kind of friend is each of us?

LW: Who are the important people in your life and what makes them important?

JORY: For the people that I've known the longest, it's definitely that they were willing to put up with the challenges. When we moved to South Carolina, I was five, and James, who lived down the street, was also five. And only a limited subset of five-year-olds would be willing to put up with me, and it just happened to be the case that James was one of those subsets. The same with Nancy, who is our neighbor across the street. I don't really recall this, but I've heard this from other people that she put in a lot of time coming over and essentially allowing me to get used to her. The first few times Mom left me at her house, I was very unhappy with that arrangement, and it took some time for that dynamic to alter. Most people would be really quite frustrated with that and not everybody would be willing to tolerate that.

Generally, I feel like I have more female friends than male friends. I've never really thought about why that's the case. Probably they are just easier to talk to. At the University of South Carolina, the majority of my mentors and friends were female. At Oxford, the people I have hung out with are less sporty—sports are huge there, some people do sports all the time. But for a lot of my friend choices I don't feel like they have anything to do with autism in particular.

LW: What makes friendship a challenge for you?
JORY: Because I'm on a different wavelength or whatever you want to call it, I don't feel like people can get to know me very well or very easily. I feel like a big part of friendship is feeling like you know a person and then you know what matters to them, and you know various things about them and how they react and what they're like. You know their personality, their values.

When you have some level of trust, then people share something that they would not have shared otherwise. It's tied into vulnerability or real thoughts. Anytime you can get to real thoughts, as opposed to small talk, or trust, or create a shared value, that is always worth it. It only happens in person too. You can maybe do it over video calling or Skype, but really in person is where you get those things, at least as I've found it.

I don't really form first impressions. The picture is always going to start off really bad because it takes me a while. I can carry on a conversation with almost anyone, but as far as feeling like I know that person, well, to get from that basic level to anything else, it probably takes about seven or eight separate interactions of at least twenty to thirty minutes, and only after a few months will I know some stuff about them.

LW: Why do you feel that separation from other people? Why do you think it is such a challenge for them to get to know you or you to get to know them?

JORY: The best way I can describe it is as sort of like a floating island. You can see it fine—there's not a big chasm in between. The island I'm on is really small, but you're not there. You're still on your island. I can see you and you can see me—and we can order telescopes and see each other in detail. But it's different because we're not standing on the same ground. And while there isn't that much difference, it's still different ground. Some differences are not going to be intelligible to either side because we don't have a soil sampler that can reach across the chasm. We only have things like telescopes or other methods of observation.

LW: Are you saying that our two islands were created by the same volcano and that, if you drill down, we will share the soil sample? Or are you saying that my island was created by a different volcano and my soil sample is never going to match up with yours? That while it might look the same—and while our islands might look the same from each of our telescopes—we are not actually standing on the same ground.

JORY: Even islands created from the same volcanic blast drift apart on geologic time. Part of me wants to say yeah, it's a different volcano and so it's a vastly different chemical signature. Then there's another part that says well, I'm not so sure, it could be the same volcano, but separate eruptions that created two distinct masses, with one mass—yours—being significantly bigger.

For you, everybody's on the same island, and you have all these things that make communication easier. You have the subconscious, social contracts, and culture and the meanings of language, which everybody knows about. You might not have to think about it, because if everybody around you is not thinking about it, then why bother thinking about it yourself?

LW: Do you think it would be hard to have a very emotional friend? Are you drawn to people who are more logical and restrained?

JORY: It's super ironic but I think I actually communicate fairly well with both types. The more emotional-type person usually considers me a really great listener, and that's because I have no idea what's going on with them. And I do probably listen well. So that's pretty hilarious. My responses are hilariously optimal because I ask them to elaborate on their feelings or I just kind of say oh, thank you very much for sharing.

With people who are not emotional, I don't usually bring up emotions, we just talk about cool stuff. So it meshes with them too. Through no intention or skill on my own behalf, I tend to be reasonably okay communicating with a cross section of people.

If you're kind of bad at communicating anyway, it's not like you're better at communicating with one specific group of people and you gravitate toward them. I'm bad at communicating with anyone, but other people don't really notice that. They think I'm very uniform in how I communicate with people, but it's that I have a pretty low level across the board.

LW: What mystifies you about friendship?

JORY: One thing I find very hard to grasp is why in any situation—even if you were trying to "get ahead"—you would treat another person as a means to an end rather than as an end in themselves. The logical thing would be that people prefer to be treated as an end to themselves and not as a rung on someone else's ladder. But I think quite a lot of people actually see conversations and interactions with people as being a means to some end. It's very confusing because the goal is disturbing. Is it a choice? I don't think it's a choice, because people don't really think about it. But it begs the question—what part of your brain is deciding that for you?

Why you will not find Jory networking:

JORY: I definitely feel like in many ways I'm not the typical Rhodes Scholar profile. I have difficulty networking because it's a social environment. Every few months, Rhodes House will have Meet and Mingles, which is exactly what it sounds like. Everybody's in one room and you mingle. It's just not something that I really do. As a result, I know numerically less people than some of the other scholars. But on the other hand, I feel like I actually know the Rhodes Scholars that I hang out with and play board games with pretty well. And the coding group I joined, and a few other people who I intentionally try to meet up with on a semi-regular basis. And the porters and staff at Rhodes House. That might be about a dozen people, but I feel like I've gotten to know them, and we have conversations that are really meaningful and interesting.

I've interacted with the community less than other people, but I feel like I've had a lot of value to the interactions that I have had. So I don't think I would really change anything. Because it's not like you could ever make a Meet and Mingle super open or friendly to somebody with autism. But they should definitely still run them.

Talking about the Value of an Autistic Person:

Differences and deficits frequently dominate a conversation about autism. But one thing Jory is very clear on is that he would not change his present state. I asked him, in various ways, to discuss the value of autism and also how relevant the concept of autism is to him as he engages with the world.

LW: How do you perceive autism in terms of both yourself as an individual and in terms of the larger stereotypes that exist?
JORY: Finishing college and going to Oxford brought me to a realization that I'm not ever going to let myself be defined by other people because I have autism or any other disability. It's not arrogant to me. I already know who I am. It's just, you don't understand some things about me in the same way that I don't

understand things about you. But that also doesn't mean that we can't have a shared vision or act collectively toward a goal.

It's a good thing to recognize people for their talents, and I definitely think that in many cases the people called autistic savants are amazing by any measure at what they do—piano or math or whatever it is. That's something unique and really nice to value. I feel like as long as it doesn't become "Oh, this autistic person isn't a savant, therefore they're less valuable," it's fine.

I'm not at an extra level in any one particular thing like that. But that doesn't mean that I think of myself as having a less talented version of autism or I'm not as smart, right?

But "autistic savant" has an almost positive stereotype associated with it. People are witnessing something so magical that the benefits outweigh the differences, whereas when they see other people with autism, they focus on the differences and not the benefits. They don't see them as easily or maybe don't consider them to be beneficial.

Jory shares his definition of autistic empathy and explains why he thinks that empathy does not have to be emotional:

JORY: Probably the other most common stereotype is that autistic people experience emotions differently, so they don't have empathy, which is an interesting one. For something like empathy, most people think of empathy in a cultural way: I empathize with you because I have felt that before, and it brings to mind my memories and that feeling, so I can connect it to what you must be feeling. And that's empathy. I can't really do that. But I don't think that process fully encompasses empathy.

I think there is logical empathy, maybe you can call it. It's an empathy that's not based on an emotion, but is based on thinking. I may not be able to fully understand someone else's situation emotionally, but I still can reason through and think about it in depth and in a detailed way, probably more than many other people do because they're caught up in the emotional connection. If anything, I also think that's more permanent as well. If it's emotional, it kind of burns brightly but then it fades away. But if you think about something, it sticks with you. And I've found that I think about it in depth later, when I'm not in the same setting and not interacting with that person anymore.

I think with autism stereotypes, people often assume, "Oh, they're bad at this thing that normal people do all the time." But that stereotype, while it may be correct, also misses out on the things that I'm good at. I've seen very little public consideration for a logical empathy, which is more nuanced, where it's possible to be good at one part of it and bad at another part of it.

LW: There are a lot of lists speculating on different historical and more contemporary figures who may have been autistic. The names include Thomas Jefferson, Albert Einstein, Steve Jobs, Michelangelo, Mozart, Isaac Newton, and Nikola Tesla. What are your thoughts when you see lists like that and people making the case that these individuals also may have been on the autism spectrum?
JORY: I don't particularly know why anybody would be overly concerned about that. To me, Tesla's scientific accomplishments are interesting, but I wouldn't be interested in whether he did or didn't have autism. Same with everyone else. I might glance at it, but that's all.

I have noticed that a journalist I follow on Twitter had #autistic in his Twitter bio. I clicked on it and found out it is a thing that people on the spectrum use to signify that they are on the spectrum. I don't know if I would ever do that because it doesn't seem like the most important thing about me.

LW: Why wouldn't you do it? Does it make you uncomfortable, or do you think, This is not relevant?

JORY: It's not relevant to me personally—in my opinion it's emotional rhetoric and I don't find it appealing or convincing. But I do think it's helpful in the same way that a lot of social movements like Me Too are. I'm certain that a lot of males I know did not know the extent to which that was an issue until so many women were posting it in their Facebook feeds, for instance. In that sense, I think it's very valuable and that hashtag, #autism, might be really valuable. People would click on it and find it's just a bunch of people with autism that do normal-people things, like write for a newspaper. In a way, perhaps that is the point of saying, what about all these smart people like Einstein or Tesla or Steve Jobs, what if they had autism? Maybe that's helpful, and it's at least not negative. I might roll my eyes a little bit, but if it's positive coverage, that's probably good in the long run.

I think a decent percentage of the people in the US and elsewhere are afraid of autism. Positive stuff probably does help marginally to fight against that.

LW: Would you put #autism in your Twitter bio?

JORY: I don't think I would. Right now, I'm more likely to list the subject areas I have studied. I suppose I might at some point use the hashtag. But what's interesting is that in order to do that, I'd have to delete something else, and I wouldn't want to delete what I have, at least not right now. Because it's a choice. You only have X number of characters in your Twitter bio.

LW: Would it frustrate you if #autism became your shorthand bio—if your life became seen as that hashtag?

JORY: Not particularly, no. I don't really think that hard about what other people think about me, to be honest. I think it's helpful from a leadership/ethics perspective to be aware of how other people generally think of you and, in particular, whether they think something you've decided or done was bad or sucks. That's helpful to pay attention to. But otherwise, I don't really pay attention at all. So, I will check for feedback from people to make sure I'm not being an idiot or being mean or have made a really bad decision. But other than that, I don't let other people define me when I already have defined myself.

LW: I was talking with a young, autistic adult whose father told him there's "no way someone diagnosed with autism can be a Rhodes Scholar." If someone said that to you, how would you respond?

JORY: With two facts: I have autism, and I am a Rhodes Scholar. At Oxford, I didn't take a place from somebody else. If my interview panel didn't like me, they could have picked someone else. There were ten or eleven other people that they interviewed that day who were equally qualified. It's not like they didn't have other options if they didn't like me when they spoke to me.

I'm sure over one hundred years, at least one other Rhodes

Scholar must have had autism; they just were never diagnosed with it. So while it may be a statistically small number, it's still possible. But what would be the functional utility of somebody saying no one who is autistic can be a Rhodes Scholar? In my case, I do happen to be a Rhodes Scholar, so it has happened. I would want to know the reason behind the statement.

LW: What are five things that you appreciate or would not change about having autism?

JORY: That's a good one. It's tough because in individual circumstances these things can be good or bad. But I feel like I would keep lack of understanding of emotions because I feel like it leads to less reliance on emotions. I've seen scenarios where emotion creates problems, and where from my end, it would not be a problem if you solved things like I solve things. Because I'm on a different playing field from other people, if somebody ever did want to be adversarial against me, they really couldn't use a lot of emotional weapons because they are very ineffective.

I think emotions are kind of weaponized too frequently, very unfortunately. I may miss the parts of emotional intelligence, but I see enough of them being weaponized to think maybe not having them be very important to me is working.

The second one I would keep is my mind working differently. Operating on a different playing field is helpful because other people can explain to me the things that are happening, and I can get double the information. And I love stockpiling information. It's one of the things I just enjoy doing, just acquiring new facts every day. Being on a different plane doubles that.

The language bit I would not keep because I would like to

communicate better with language. I also would not keep the autistic behaviors bit—what's known as "stimming"—because I'll find myself doing random things with my hands and I'm not even aware of it. Like messing with my hair. I could delete that. We're only at two. I'm trying to think what else there is.

I would want to keep the hard experiences because I think that those are valuable as teaching moments. Just the other day there was a nursery rhyme, and Mom was saying, "Oh, you don't know X rhyme?" I'm like, No. I know really very, very few nursery rhymes because that is not part of my memory. But not having those earlier memories makes the later ones comparatively more important in a weird way. Because a lot of what I know is more recent, it results in it being more accessible. So I don't remember nursery rhymes, but maybe because I don't have nursery rhymes in my brain, maybe that space is being used for marine science and ocean stuff. Who knows if that's true or not? But if it is true, then I'd want to keep that. I also feel like because those earlier times were more difficult and because I wasn't interacting with more people, then interactions that I did have were pretty meaningful, like with my family and with James and Miss Nancy. I feel like having a more limited set of interactions earlier on meant that they were more valuable as well. That taught me very useful life things about the importance of family and close friends and things of that nature.

The reason why I was in Oxford as a Rhodes Scholar is my obsession with trying to fix some of the world's problems. I would be most unhappy in a position, even if I was making a lot of money, where I didn't feel like I was fixing something or improving the general state of things. That early experience of having those few but very important linkages puts things in perspective.

Explaining Autistic Behaviors

For as long as I can remember, I have had what are called "autistic behaviors," some of which are known by the word *stimming*. I will pull my hair or hold my hands up to my face or in front of my mouth while I talk, or bend my elbows and flap my hands, or suck on my fingers, or start singing a nonsense song in random places. For a number of years, when I was younger, I also pulled on my lip to the point where it bled, moderately to severely. Lip tissue is very fragile and hard to heal, so that was going to have real consequences for my health. That habit was difficult to break. Other people do these behaviors to varying degrees, but often for very different reasons.

I recall practicing a presentation on climate change, and my mother and my sister were my audience, and they both noticed that I was pulling on my hair and generally messing with my hair and holding my hands up to my face as I spoke. But I wasn't aware that I was doing any of those things, I wasn't even thinking about it. And I wasn't doing them because I was nervous. Rather, I was concentrating so hard that I didn't have the mental energy to think about not doing those automatic movements. Otherwise, I do have to make an effort at what's called masking, an effort to consciously control these involuntary behaviors.

Neurotypical people might look at them and interpret that I am nervous, but in fact that's not it at all. The more I'm doing nervous-looking behavior, the more I'm inside my mind, thinking and concentrating. I'm also more likely to do these things in a stressful environment with a lot of stimuli or when I'm really distracted.

For instance, if I'm in a grocery store with bright lights and way too many choices of pasta, I can find that environment stressful, and I end up singing a nonsense song to Daisy. When I watch a movie in a theater, or when I sit on the sofa at home with my family and watch an episode of *Schitt's Creek* or *The Office*, I often end up sucking on my fingers, because I'm distracted by what I'm watching, and I don't think about what else I'm doing. I've also sometimes started sucking on my fingers in a lecture hall while I'm very focused on what the professor is saying. But I try to be self-aware enough to stop that quickly. At home or at the movies, Mom may have to remind me not to do it, even occasionally pulling my fingers out of my mouth. I can't say for sure why this happens, but these behaviors seem to be triggered by that inner brain machinery that runs on autopilot.

When I'm out in public, I do have to work to consciously not engage in these behaviors. I've changed hand flapping to fiddling with pens or holding Daisy's leash. I can mess with pens or the leash or some other small object, because that is more acceptable. I still may sing a nonsense song in the grocery store, but I try to turn down the volume.

I know that neurotypical people sometimes engage in some of these behaviors too. They may mess with their hair or bite their fingernails or chew on their lips or hold up their hands, but it seems that they are able to modify that behavior or dial it back a lot more smoothly than people with autism. It's a bit like a musical composition, where different notes go together. When neurotypical people do these things, there's something about it that doesn't seem discordant or off, it blends. But when an autistic person engages in these behaviors, it has a different sound. It's more like a bad note in a symphony, it's jarring and stops the whole thing. Because I do care how people view me, I do try to notice if I'm doing something weird and ask myself, Is this a problem? Should I be caring about the outcome?

I'm not going to become something else just to enter the path to faith that most people believe is the correct path. Because that would be denying who I am, which from a Christian context is like denying your own journey of healing and becoming a better version of yourself.

Something that really speaks to me personally is the Christian message. In terms of language, I feel almost like God thought of this in my case. Because the message is just one word. *Love.* You know. Straight from Jesus. Which is great, because how awesome is it that you only need one word to get the message? The core message is just one word. I'm like, Aha! Fewer words is a good thing. For somebody with autism, I very much appreciate that really there's only one word that's at the core. I feel like it was a hip bonus perhaps just for people with autism. One word. You got it.

LW: What are the foundations of your relationship with God and your faith? How do you describe that relationship?

JORY: I feel in some sense that I may get some supernatural assistance from God and from my faith. People ask me why I tend to be generally undisturbed by the fact that, compared to somebody else, my life might suck—according to their perspective, I might add; I think it's kind of fine from my perspective. But I've never felt that way because while there are negative aspects in some ways, there are also positive aspects. And they both are present at the same time. But one is more important than the other: the positive elements. It interests me that a lot of elements of society are focused perhaps too much on those negative aspects, and they don't focus on the positive aspects.

From other people's perspective, it might be difficult to imag-

9

One Word: *LOVE*

Talking about Faith:

Jory is a person of faith. We spoke about his views on faith, about how it has sustained him, what perspective it gives him, and why he believes so deeply in God. "If you do believe in a Creator, then by default, you would also have to believe that the Creator would know very well his own handiwork," he says. God, in other words, created Jory. He is not an aberration, but a considered choice.

Jory also very much believes that individual faith does not need to be driven by emotion. His faith is driven by logic.

JORY: Somebody once freaked out when I said that my faith was 100 percent logical. But it's true, it has no emotional base; it's totally logical and analytical. That's due to the fact of autism, but I feel like that in no way diminishes it. If anything, maybe that will show people their perceptions of possible paths is limited when they shouldn't be limited. The relationship we have with God doesn't have to be built on emotion alone.

ine why, for someone who is a scientist and with all these medical problems, faith is such an important area to turn to. But for me, it's not only reaffirmed and shaped what I want to do with my life, but it has also been very practical in my method of thinking.

The way my mind works is in some ways much more "equational," if that's a word, than other people's. To get by and understand people, I try to process things I'm observing and compute what that might mean. But I know human meaning can't be encapsulated by equations, and that's why I go to chapel all the time.

I feel like faith is also interesting in terms of relationships. I'm always going to be bad at any relationship that I have. But there's at least one that's going to be a very good relationship.

If you do believe in a Creator, then by default, you would also have to believe that the Creator would know very well his own handiwork.

My relationship with my Creator is a relationship that I don't have to work at much at all. For every other relationship, there are different gradations, from family through friends, to people that I know, to strangers, and the difficulty increases with each one. With people, I don't understand what goes in and what comes out, and how to relate.

But I can always reconnect with my relationship with my Creator.

I've met a few people from various religions. Not terribly many. But there's one other person I can think of off the top of my head in particular that is a Christian and two others that are Muslim and one that's Hindu. They all have a sense of peace about them. I feel in some regard faith and religion make you think about things beyond yourself. You think about society and helping others. Not that people without religion can't do that. They certainly do. But for me, my faith is important for me in terms of how I function. It's useful to sort of have a wider perspective on the world and life and values that are going to stick with you.

This leads us into a conversation about the role of faith on life's journey, and specifically in Jory's journey.

JORY: The highest point in South Carolina is a mountain, but it's really kind of a big hill, and it's a several-hour hike to the top. For me, it's harder than it would be for a super-fit person. I always think about how much effort it takes to get up the first half of the hill, and then about halfway or two-thirds of the way up, I've reached the maximum state of tiredness, so I don't feel tired anymore. I've gotten used to being tired, so I'm not thinking about going up step-by-step and all the energy required. And the second part is that I'm focused on the destination.

It's the larger point that the journey is bearable if the destination is known and worth it. This climb, which might be trivial for someone else, is meaningful for you.

I also feel like there is a faith element to it as well. In a number of faith traditions, not just Christianity, the journey that is life is made more magical by knowing the elements of your destination. I feel like at times I'm able to off-load some of that extra effort through my faith, through the idea that the Holy Spirit is supposedly present with you at all times. When I think about the scale of what my mind has to do, what it has to do manually that other people just do automatically, it should be way too much effort for me to have any energy left over to think about any complex topic.

LW: Pull out some Jory beads and give me your mental image of faith, please.

JORY: I have this picture of the concept of faith in general, across churches and religions, as being like a kelp plant. Kelp has a specialized rootlike structure called the holdfast, and it latches on to a rock or something on the bottom of the sea, so it's got a nice anchor. But then it floats all the way up to the top of the water. The leaves have little air sacs that help it stay afloat. It's holding fast to something rooted and it's also free in the waves and experiencing the varying currents of change and motion and the whims of the surface. It changes and shifts, but it also doesn't. It just depends on your perspective.

LW: Do you pray, and what do you pray about?

JORY: Yes. At Oxford, I started going to Morning Prayer chapel services, which are at eight fifteen, because it's an interesting way to start the day. I enjoy it, even though I absolutely detest mornings normally.

The Church of England is interesting as well because it's more liturgical than other denominations I've been part of. In Morning Prayer, certain elements will always be the same, so you can get familiar and comfortable with them. There's one that talks about how the night has passed, the day lies open before us. It's just a factual statement, but it is interesting, the day does lie open before us. Being in England, it's often a cloudy, rainy day, but it's still a new day and anything can happen. You get reminded of useful tidbits like that. An extra bonus.

For myself, I tend to pray for my interactions with other people because it's something I'm concerned with because I'm not very good at it, and I know negative things can come from my poor performance. That's important for me. With prayer, you know you're not saying anything new, if you are of the mind that your prayer is being heard. There's nothing new on the other end of the religious telephone line, so to speak.

During prayer, I'll also try to think of other people and something that may be happening in their lives. The days are so busy that, as horrible as it is, I might forget about things. One of the few things that my brain does automatically is prioritize information in terms of storage, so I find it hard to remember people's names and faces and things like that.

But if somebody confides in me something that they're concerned about, I want to remember, because the next time I see them I want to remember what they told me, and we had this interaction that was meaningful and not just say, "How's the weather today?" which is something that I don't like at all. To do that, I have to prioritize that information. If the day is busy, I don't have time to actively remember. So I pray for people because I care about them and want them to receive comfort, but also so that I can remember. And try to override my subconscious prioritization that would de-prioritize that human information. Because what I do all the time is take all this human information floating around, and for the most part, I redirect it and shunt it away so that I can function better. But there are times where you want to capture some of that information as well.

LW: You mentioned to me the scriptural mandate to protect the weak, which is one of the tenets of Christianity, and in different ways, of other religions as well. How do you view that mandate? What does it look like through your eyes?

JORY: I've been thinking about the stereotype that if you lack emotion, you're cold and calculating. But that perspective doesn't necessarily make me cold and calculating. Maybe it is in fact a better way to fulfill the scriptural mandate to protect the weak. Many people react emotionally to weakness. But the scriptural advice, not just from Christianity but from other religions, is that the weak can have surprisingly different sources of strength. From my experience, I'm weak in all sorts of ways, but I've been able to positively contribute.

Part of problem solving is about understanding and presence, because I have witnessed instances where I have no solutions for any emotional problem, but I can try to understand, be present, and that is often an interaction which creates meaning. While I understand less, the fact that I observe more, the fact that I, in my small way, learn something each time is really valuable for me and hopefully for other people as well. Sometimes the answer is not a solution but just presence or an attempt at understanding.

I know other people have a better understanding than me, that they have a really super-advanced radar. Whereas mine is terrible, but at least it's working hard all the time.

Talking about a Philosophy of Life:

Initially, this project was conceived as a memoir of Jory's mind, and the story of what he has overcome and achieved. But as our conversations grew deeper, it evolved. The story became less about what Jory has done in spite of autism and more about who Jory is because of autism. How he sees life, how he approaches it, how his perspective and inner compass came to be are inseparable from his condition. To accurately convey Jory, the talking, the back-and-forth, and the exchange of ideas became invaluable. I wanted to put readers in my shoes, to ask questions you might ask, then listen and respond (and reflect) as you would. For Jory, I wanted to build the safe space that he finds missing, to metaphorically get in my own boat and row as close to his island as I could.

From this place, we found ourselves discussing not simply language and processing and the reading and misreading of emotion but fundamental characteristics of what makes us, the nearly eight billion of us on planet Earth, human. And what might make us better as humans.

A young man who struggles every day to understand people around him has pierced to the heart of some of the most fundamental dilemmas facing us in the twenty-first century. Have we considered the long-term consequences of embracing emotional drama and fervent rhetoric and allowing them to play such dominant roles? Have we given sufficient regard to the value and practice of critical thinking? Are we willing to make space for diversity of thought? A young man who is forced to husband his own mental energy has observed the rest of us and wonders if many of the things that we neurotypicals expend our brain energy on are superfluous or even harmful. Is it not better, instead, he ventures, for each of us to commit, "from [our] own internal space," to correcting the imbalances we see in the world?

How might we begin to rebalance those imbalances? Much like his personality choice of ruthless optimism, Jory is a proponent of practical idealism. He advocates for smart people to do less thinking and more real-world problem solving. As for managing the level of anger in our current debates, he proposes an autistic circuit breaker for "normal people."

The title for this section, "A Philosophy of Life," was chosen with much thought and care. In terms of personal burdens and challenges, life dealt Jory a very difficult hand. But then, for his next card, he drew an ace in the form of self-awareness. That awareness is his gift to share as many of us search for ways to navigate an ever-more fractured society. When Jory speaks of how "you, me, each of us has the internal stability to be able to stand against the tide of the world," this thoughtful man who relies on leg braces knows exactly how hard it is to remain upright amid the buffeting waves and constantly shifting sands.

JORY: There's a phrase that I've heard, which I think is very appropriate here. Too often, emotion-based conversations devolve into "throwing dirt." But throwing dirt is not helpful, because not only do you get your hands dirty, but you are losing ground. You aren't making positive progress toward something; you are just throwing back more emotional words in someone else's face. No one is learning or improving their understanding of a problem.

I listen to people say that vaccines cause autism or things like that. It's hard to understand their fear, so I would try to ask questions. Are you afraid of me? Why is that? When I get people to question a premise and then turn on some semblance of critical thinking, it reverses. For a good number of people, it is possible to reverse the effects of mass manipulation. The real solution would be to teach people critical thinking in school. Everything about society is set up to avoid critical thinking and to get you sucked into a routine and ideology-based groups that make things comfortable for you. Critical thinking is often very uncomfortable, at least in my opinion. You have to reevaluate yourself, which means that, heaven forbid, you might be wrong sometimes.

Most people don't like neutral. They want you to have an opinion. And I've always been of the mind that opinions are only useful if you're willing to change them very rapidly. I feel like the stronger your opinion, the weaker you should hold it. Mom will tell you that I am strongly opinionated, but I would say that I do actually change my mind on things. I am quite curious about the other side of an argument. In a lot of cases, people think that means you have no values. But that's just people confusing values and opinions.

A value is something that has to be tied to philosophy and systems and ethics. Whereas an opinion can be more emotional and tied on to your individual assessment of a situation, which could be correct or could be wrong.

LW: How do you define freedom of thought and why is it so important to you?

JORY: I feel like what I'll be able to accomplish in my life will be necessarily limited by the fact that I'm just one individual, but I do have the freedom to decide my internal fate. You, me, each of us has the internal stability to be able to stand against the tide of the world.

Maintaining that internal stability to stand against the tide is emblematic of a greater freedom, which I feel everybody has. It is what freedom of thought entails, the freedom that nobody can enter your mind, at least not yet—we still don't have that kind of spooky AI [artificial intelligence]. Individual thought is a strong, irreversible force. It's one of the few irreversible things, in my opinion.

Diversity of thought is also really valuable as an aggregate. Every person agreeing with every other person, that would be conformity. And conformity is usually not resilient, whereas diversity is more resilient. We're never going to agree, but we can find common meaning. You can look at someone and say, "Oh, that person has those qualities and finds these things important, and their journey through life will never occur exactly that way again."

You have a set of tools available to you, which are uniquely yours and are empowered, because each person has unique disabilities and abilities. That should be highly valued.

If you have your tools and your thoughts, then you have what's necessary to make the change that you want to see happen in the world. Or at least to try. No guarantee you're going to succeed, but you can at least go for it.

LW: You are very committed to changing the world. How can one individual or a few individuals working together achieve that kind of change? Where does it start?

JORY: In college, I helped lead a class where I was basically mentoring people on how to be mentors. It was creating a chain reaction of mentorship. I was working with a co-instructor to help students work through problems, where we got to lead by example. Leading by example is something that I think is extremely valuable and very underutilized. You can look at some leaders and realize not everyone should lead by example. I see it with emotions. People respond to emotions with their own emotions. Or they respond to an ethical deficit base by not being ethical themselves. That's incredible to me.

We live in a world where there are power structures that people create, which hold other people down. If you do nothing, then you are maintaining the status quo, right? If bad things are happening, why wouldn't you respond?

If you think lack of kindness is a problem, why would you try to tackle that problem with your own lack of kindness? From your internal space, decide how you want to correct the imbalances you see in the world. And having no response is also a response. That is a choice as well.

Problems are not solved by doing the same thing over and over again or by trying to solve one problem by applying another problem. Instead, you have to identify the problem and develop a solution. It also doesn't have to always be your solution, right? It can be shared knowledge, a shared creation. But to do that, you have to put in a lot of hard work. You have to have a lot of communication. You have to build up everybody so that they can freely participate.

One thing that I think is fortunate about autism for me is that I'm so amorphous. I can relate to where everyone's coming from in a way that other people who are latched on to ideologies or latched on to culture or latched on to their identities can't. They can't quite experience that. It's almost like being so amorphous has resulted in my being empathetic, not in an emotional sense, but more in an intellectual sense.

Jory talks about the problem of anger in how we address our problems as individuals and as a society, and also in our public discourse.

JORY: I can name facts that happened over six months ago, and people draw a blank. But I don't blank on such things; I can't ignore them. And I don't really know how to translate that to other people.

But I do wish people would take a moment and take in things happening around them. It's a mindset you have to practice all the time, like did you smell that flower or like why are you walking so fast? Or why are you arguing with this person about a totally meaningless topic, or why is this weird negative emotion building up inside of you out of nowhere because of spilled milk? It's crazy.

I finally deleted Facebook off my phone because there was too much political arguing, just repeating the same points over and over, like an infinite loop, where no one's mind was being changed and no one was adding new or useful facts. It was all people searching for ways to repeat the opinions they already had.

Sometimes I look around and think, lots of people are not very good at interacting with other people. They may think that autism is a disability, but at least I'm aware of the fact that I don't interact with people very well. I see so much anger, and I feel like saying, "You know what, y'all are disabled too. You just don't know it because you're all the same."

I know that I can't change X problem or issue, and you probably can't change X either, but you can change the next time you want to feel angry.

Take like a five-second mental loop and ask yourself why you want to feel angry and who's trying to make you feel angry, and a bunch of other questions that might make you less angry. I know it's really hard for people to do that. I've seen them go through it. It's like it happens so quickly that you don't even have time to ask yourself that one mental question before you're already on to being angry about the next thing.

But people need to install something like a circuit breaker to stop this crazy amount of emotion. I need to design an autistic circuit breaker for normal people.

LW: One of the "selling points" for artificial intelligence is the idea that it's not emotion-based. Instead, it's described as being rational and making different calculations. Does that sound to you as being a little like how autism is described—or at least having that same freedom from emotion?

JORY: One of the things that I see from an autistic perspective are the dangers inherent to ideology and emotion. But I wouldn't go so far as to say that a completely rational artificial intelligence, removing all emotion, would be best for people without autism. I actually think it would break people if they weren't controlled by emotion or ideology. I don't think people would be strong enough to deal with that.

LW: Why?

JORY: If all of a sudden you just take away the strengths that people have, they're left only with their weaknesses. I've had to deal with my weaknesses and build up my strengths. But to take away somebody else's strength just because it's my weakness is not right. Some projections say that 10 percent to almost 50 percent of human tasks could be automated in the next hundred years. It will probably have a pretty decent effect, but it also could just change everything. And it's too early to say. But the problem is that the decisions are not being made with enough forethought to other elements, like, ironically for me to say, emotion.

Because yes, it might be more efficient and create more wealth in an economic sense if everything's automated, but if nobody has a job, you need to prepare for that. And many of the jobs that will be created from this are going to be high-paying jobs that need both high skills and high education, and those jobs may not be going to people with disabilities, people with tough backgrounds, or people who have worked in different jobs.

People are not very good at dealing with the intersection of technology and the human condition. They say, "Oh, we'll just retrain everybody." It's really insulting to tell someone whose lifestyle was upended by forces far removed from them and very much beyond their control, "Get some counseling and job retraining and you'll be good to go."

I don't think anybody would say that the state of the world now is worse than in the 1700s, for example. But that doesn't mean that we are invincible going forward.

LW: How do you see your life going forward? What matters to you? What principles do you hope will guide you?
JORY: I don't want to be one of those people that just kind of sits in the back and thinks about things. I love doing that, but I think there are too many of those people. More of the smart people should do less of the thinking, which is kind of paradoxical.

But at some point, you have to stop thinking and get moving. You've got to pick something you want to work on and try to do it.

There are trees in Oxford that have been here for longer than the US has existed. But you also have all the flowers which are here one day and gone the next. It's a sense of beauty, which is kind of like an individual person. Because people are also here one day and gone the next. People always think they're going to live longer than they do. But that's no guarantee for anybody in particular.

Nature is a good example of thinking about that in a positive context. I'm not going to be the stately tree that's going to be around forever, but maybe some of the ideas and things I can do for the world could have a lasting impact that goes beyond my lifetime.

But even if I don't achieve the legacy of a tree, I can absolutely achieve the memorable joy of a flower, where I can try my best to have positive interactions with people and help people when they are sad or dealing with those pesky emotion things. They are things that will be forgotten but still mean something. We shouldn't ignore the wonders of the flower *or* the stately tree; we should focus on both.

At the end of the day, we are all just living on the planet. If you actually think about it, we always have to depend on others and on the entire biological and ecological system. We as humans don't even make our own oxygen. I'm not self-sufficient. You're not self-sufficient. Nobody's self-sufficient.

A Note on Sources

Research, thinking, and writing on the brain and autism change at a remarkable rate, and all the sources below helped to inform and enrich this book by providing both general knowledge and some specific information. For a brief history of evolving views on the brain and the heart, see an essay by Stephen W. A. Reynolds of the University of Calgary, "The historical struggle for dominance between the heart, liver, and brain," given at Calgary's sixteenth annual History of Medicine Days in 2007. A detailed discussion of emotions and brain science, physiology, and culture can be found in Lisa Feldman Barrett's *How Emotions Are Made: The Secret Life of the Brain* (Mariner Books, 2017). For more information on research in juvenile brain imaging with autism, see the journal *Cerebral Cortex*, Volume 29, Issue 6, June 2019. The journal *Science* published a paper on the relationship between the gut and the brain, "A Gut Feeling," by Benjamin Hoffman and Ellen Lumpkin on September 21, 2018. And the US National Library of Medicine at the National Institutes of Health offers a detailed compendium of articles and studies on autism and brain research, including Catherine Wan and Gottfried Schlaug's "Neural pathways for language in autism: the potential for music-based treatments." Finally, two general interest books: *In A Different Key: The Story of Autism* by John Donvan and Caren Zucker (Broadway Books, 2016), which comprehensively traces our collective recognition of, understanding of, and reaction to autism, and *The Tale of the Dueling Neurosurgeons: The History of the Human Brain as Revealed By True Stories of Trauma, Madness, and Recovery* by Sam Kean (Back Bay Books, 2014), which explores how medicine and science came to better understand the brain. A 2019 adaptation of the novel *The Curious Incident of the Dog in the Nighttime* at the Round House Theatre in Bethesda, Maryland, sparked much additional thought about how to translate and navigate between two intellectual worlds. And a note on punctuation: Because Jory does not think in words, to remain true and consistent to his mind, no quotes were used to refer to his thoughts, unless they were spoken out loud.

Acknowledgments

This book is the result of many who have helped me on my journey thus far.

To my family, who have always been there ever since I can remember. To Mom, Lauren, Arich, Sarah, Tyler, Ruth, Nancy, and Herb. Thanks to Federer and Daisy.

The writing of this book could be its own story, and it would include many who helped bring it to life for you, the reader. I was initially overwhelmed that anyone would find my story worth reading about, and I'd like to thank Elliot Gerson and Walter Isaacson for helping me navigate the initial process. Amanda Urban has been a tremendous support and guide over the past two years. I especially want to thank Lyric Winik for helping me speak to others in a language that is not my own. I too enjoyed our conversations, and I hope to have many more.

The team at Simon & Schuster has been instrumental in making this book a reality. I'd like to thank my editor, Priscilla Painton, who saw a story and moved mountains so that you can read it today. Thank you for your belief, support, and vision in making this book come to life. Sincere thanks to Simon & Schuster CEO Jonathan Karp for his faith that I had something to say. Thanks as well to Richard Rhorer, vice president and deputy publisher, for his personal interest and support. And thank you to all at S&S who shepherded this book: Hana Park and Megan Hogan in editorial, who both answered every question; Carly Loman for her thoughtful interior design; cover designer Jackie Seow; production editor Sara Kitchen; copyeditor Tricia Callahan; and publicity/marketing leads Anne Tate Pearce and Elise Ringo.

There have been so many that have helped me over the years, and it would be impossible to name them all, but I will try to share some of their names with you. First, to James Jacocks, my oldest, and for a long time only, friend.

There were many therapists who assisted me with my various disabilities, and I'd like to thank them now because I definitely didn't at the time. Thank you to Karen Timmons, my physical therapist for many years, who always built me up (both literally and figuratively). Thanks to everyone who invested in me when I was younger, especially Dennie Sides and Vic and Joan Jones.

Thanks to Jen Rogers, Maureen Leary, and everyone in the PAALS family. Daisy has been my constant companion and a continual reminder of how many people gave their time and love to my journey.

I found a home at the University of South Carolina full of friends who supported me in every way. Thanks to Jean Ellis, Joe Jones, Hamid Khan, David Taylor, and David DeWeil for being mentors as well as friends. To Cocky and everyone at Cocky's Reading Express, I promise to try and live every day with the joy you showed me. To Novella Beskid, the Office for National Fellowships and Scholar

Programs, and everyone in the UofSC family who supported me during both my time in Columbia and the United Kingdom.

I'd like to thank Andrew Rich and Tara Yglesias of the Truman Foundation. I am very grateful for all you did for me.

My time at Oxford was transformative in many ways. Thank you to Mary Eaton and all the staff at Rhodes House (especially the porters) for welcoming Mom and me. The reason I popped around so frequently was because our conversations gave me great joy. Thank you to all the staff, porters, and gardeners at Worcester College, for giving me a second home. Thank you to everyone at the University Church and the Oxford University Scottish Dance Society. Thank you to the staff of the School of Geography & Environment, and the librarians at the Bodleian. To Tess Kuin Lawton, Matthew Cheung Salisbury, and Thomas Allery—I tried to tell you how much you mean to me, but I don't think I will ever be able to convey that through words. I'd like to thank the National Health Service, and by extension everyone in the United Kingdom, for giving me more than two years of freedom. Thank you for welcoming me so warmly.

Lastly, to all of my friends, you know who you are. I am tremendously lucky to call so many wonderful persons my friends, and I treasure all the memories we have made and continue to make. I hope to share with others a fraction of the light I see from you whenever we speak.

—Jory Fleming

My deepest thanks to Jory Fleming and Kelly Fleming for entrusting me with their remarkable and inspiring story.

I am always grateful to work with, learn from, and be friended by Priscilla Painton, Jonathan Karp, Hana Park, Megan Hogan, Gail Ross, and, further back, Susan Moldow, Nan Graham, Larry Smith, Sara Brzowsky, and Martin Timins, as well as Pat Rodgers Lionetti. Thanks to Jo Shuffler for your always flawless transcription.

Special thanks to my parents, Jim and Lark Wallwork, for your unwavering support and for reading every page, often twice. To my dear reading family, Jean Sheeleigh, may her memory be a blessing, and Kathy and Matt Sheeleigh, as well as Cameron Sheeleigh, Katherine Albright, and Liz Murray, and my dear reading friends Molly Teas, Toby and Ury Emsellem, Robb Bunnen, Greta Van Susteren, Janet Friedman, Vanessa Badré, Diane Cannon, Leslie Barr, Elizabeth Miller, Janice Day, Maral Skelsey, Elisabeth LaMotte, Lisa Mortier, Lesley Caldicott, David and Julie Bulitt, Alison Schafer, Liz Steinglass, and Amy Kauffman, my words are better because of your thoughts. Also Inga Barry, Sophia Maroon, Rudy Khriesat, Jill Larabee, Edith Gregson, Emily Kropp Michel, Deb Swacker, and Kelly Doolan. Thanks to Mike Millen for a truly excellent edit. I could do none of this without the wonderful Grecia Carattini, thank you. And extra thanks to sweet Cree, who never left my side or lap as I typed.

I knew this story was something extraordinary when my two teenage boys would come home from school, silently set down their backpacks, tiptoe into the room, and listen as Jory and I Skyped. At the end of each conversation, they would say, "That was really interesting, especially the part about . . ." The greatest blessing and honor in my life is to be Nathaniel and BC's mom. Thank you and love you with all of my head and all of my heart.

—Lyric W. Winik

About the Authors

JORY FLEMING recently completed a Master of Philosophy in environmental change and management at the University of Oxford as a Rhodes Scholar. Prior to this he completed a Bachelor of Science in geography and marine science at the University of South Carolina. Alongside his service dog, Daisy, Jory is invested in children's education and raising awareness about disabilities. He loves the ocean and hopes to keep the planet beautiful and alive for the next generation. Jory lives with several disabilities, including autism, and enjoys speaking with others about his way of seeing the world. In his spare time, Jory is an avid bird-watcher, board game enthusiast, and Scottish country dancer. This is his first book.

LYRIC WINIK is an award-winning writer and a graduate of Princeton University with a Master of Arts from Johns Hopkins University. Passionate about education, she has volunteered in Maryland public schools for more than a decade. An avid hiker, she loves exploring the outdoors with her two sons and Lakeland terrier, Cree. *How to Be Human* is her fourteenth collaborative book.